The May Beetles

'Baba's memory is astonishing and from the point of
view of a reader, in its nuance and recall of detail,
this makes the story utterly trustworthy throughout ...
her love of life shines through at every moment.'

ROBERT MANNE

'Baba Schwartz is a storyteller whose voice is so natural you
swear you are hearing it. When it tells of her joyful discovery
of the wonders of the natural world, of human creativity
and of human beings as they come, in all sorts, into her life
as a child in Hungary, it's a voice of strong but delicate vitality.
Soon she was to suffer and witness the worst crimes known
to humankind. Yet the voice that tells of those crimes is
recognisably the same one that tells of the wonders of her
childhood. She will not renounce her fidelity to those wonders
and to the gift of happiness later, in her marriage and with her
children. That is the miracle of this book. It would not have
been possible were it not for Baba's mother and sisters,
who all suffered with her, but especially her mother.
As much as anything, *The May Beetles* is an elegy to her.'

RAIMOND GAITA

The May Beetles

MY FIRST TWENTY YEARS

Baba Schwartz

Black Inc.

Published by Black Inc.,
an imprint of Schwartz Publishing Pty Ltd
Level 1, 221 Drummond Street
Carlton VIC 3053, Australia
enquiries@blackincbooks.com
www.blackincbooks.com

National Library of Australia Cataloguing-in-Publication entry:
Schwartz, Baba, author.
The May beetles: my first twenty years / Baba Schwartz.
9781863958455 (hardback)
9781925435023 (ebook)
Schwartz, Baba—Childhood and youth.
Holocaust survivors—Biography.
Holocaust victims' families—Biography.
Holocaust, Jewish (1939–1945)—Personal narratives, Hungarian.
Holocaust, Jewish (1939–1945)—Hungary.
940.5318092

Cover design by Peter Long
Text design and typesetting by Tristan Main
All photographs from the Schwartz family collection
The endpapers feature a cross-stitched cushion cover that was buried
with Baba's family photographs during the Holocaust.

Printed in China at 1010 International.

In loving memory of
my father, Gyula,
my mother, Boeske,
and my sisters, Erna and Marta.

Preface

I wrote this memoir in 1991, a quarter of a century past, and put it aside. A couple of years ago, after the death of my beloved husband, Andor, my sons asked me to print out all my writings for them. I write all the time – diary notes, contemplations, poetry, recipes – and the result was a four-inch-thick stack of sheets. I told my sons that somewhere in that wad was a memoir of my first two decades: before, during and just after the Holocaust.

My intimate jottings were too personal for my sons to read, so my publisher son introduced me to Robert Hillman, a wonderful writer, and he agreed to work with me to refine those papers into the book you are reading now. I owe Robert a debt of gratitude: he shared his talent with me and he elevated my prose. He made this book possible.

I also thank the Black Inc. people who put this book together so lovingly. In particular, I single out Julian Welch for his sensitive and accurate editing.

It will be a pleasure for me when the printed book arrives, for I will place it on my bookshelf alongside Andor's memoir, *Living Memory*. I hope these two volumes between them will impart to my children – and maybe to those a generation or two after them – that our lives were just like their lives, that our thoughts and feelings were just like theirs. That we weren't another breed; only the times were different.

Baba Schwartz
March 2016

CHAPTER 1

Before the Beginning

On my birth certificate, issued in Hungary in 1927, I am Margit. In Australia, on letters sent to me by officials, I am Margaret. But more than Margit, and much more than Margaret, I am Baba, my name since childhood. It means 'baby', and it was what my older sister, Erna, called me after I was born. It stuck, and Baba has been my name all my life.

I was born in Nyírbátor, a town of twelve thousand inhabitants in the easternmost province of Hungary, bordering the semi-pagan backwoods of Romania to the east and the slightly more civilised land we now call Slovakia to the north. Nyírbátor sits on a plain, surrounded by farms. It was not the glory of God's creation. It was a rural town with dusty streets; trees lined the main roads – acacias, with delicious scent. It was an *ordinary* town.

But I was a child and was carried along by the emotion in my heart, and to me Nyírbátor was home. Of course, if you are loved and cared for, and your mother is what my mother was to me, your father like my father, affectionate, endlessly protective, then any town, even Nyírbátor with its dusty streets, is a paradise.

I wish to begin by talking about the first meeting of my mother and father. This was how it happened. What my father first noticed about my mother was the grace of her walk and the pleasing shape of her legs. He was on his way home from *shul*. It was late in the day, but it was early spring and there was still some light in the sky. A young woman was walking home ahead of him in a small group, tall, slender, and oh! – those legs. If her face matched the delight of her gait and the beauty of her legs, this would be a day to remember.

So he continued to follow the young woman, whose name he did not yet know, and no doubt my mother was aware that she was being followed by this fellow from *shul*, and perhaps that the grace of her walk and the shapeliness of her legs were being appraised. This man admiring my mother's legs was Gyula Keimovits, a livestock dealer, principally in cattle, who lived not quite in Nyírbátor and not quite in an outlying village but in between.

The Keimovits family's ancestral dwelling (to make it sound a little fancier than it was) was once an inn. The front part of the building was open to the public, and the living quarters for the family were at the back. Generations of the Keimovits family had sold victuals and wine in this way, and had done well enough. At some point, cattle dealing became more attractive and the living quarters took up the whole building, and anyone who needed a glass of wine had to go elsewhere.

In 1922 Gyula was twenty-six years old. A handsome man, with fair hair and blue eyes, but not educated beyond his *cheder* classes. He read Hebrew well, but he was essentially of that class of provincial European Jewish men – quite a sizeable class before the Second World War – whose members were content to know only what it was practical to know: how to live in their religion, how to honour their heritage, how to make a decent living.

Now, my father did not have the liberty to catch up with my graceful mother and propose a first date. As in all Jewish communities, Gyula relied on a *shadchan*. This matchmaker would not have been young, but she would have been a well-respected woman of some influence in the community; better if she knew how to exercise a certain amount of charm, and had developed some wisdom over the years. Very often, the *shadchan* knew everything about everybody in the community but sometimes she was simply a woman willing to accept the *mitzvah* of fashioning a meeting.

I don't know who in Nyírbátor acted as go-between for my father and my mother, but after a discreet enquiry, my mother's identity and age were revealed to Gyula. She was Erzsebet Kellner, known as Boeske; she was twenty-two years of age; she was not being courted by any other young man. Gyula learned more, some of it a little daunting. Boeske's background was more sophisticated than his: she'd been educated in Kassa, across the

3

Gyula Keimovits before marriage, circa 1920.

Hungarian border in Slovakia, a city much bigger and more beautiful than Nyírbátor. In Kassa, Boeske had learned to speak German, the hallmark of a civilised person in those days and a particular accomplishment in a young woman. And there was more: Boeske had served as secretary to the mayor of Nyírbátor from 1916 to 1918. She had met and greeted all sorts of people, many of them not of her faith; she knew how to be charming, she knew how to laugh.

Gyula had never seen Kassa and had no sophisticated friends. But he persisted, and so he should have, for what he didn't know about Boeske was that she had a serious side. She regarded the life she led, with its joking and its chatter, as a frivolous interlude. When she married, it would be to someone like Gyula: steady, reliable, generous.

It was arranged that Gyula would call on Boeske, drink tea, eat cake, enjoy some conversation, and in the process reveal the sort of man he was. And so he dressed himself in his best attire, knocked on the door of the Kellner family home in the centre of town – a big, impressive house – and asked to speak with Ignac Kellner, Boeske's father.

Gyula was welcomed into the study, where volumes of literature stood on handsome shelves next to the venerated Hebrew holy books. Ignac took him into the drawing room, where the family was gathered, including Boeske. A little polite talk: the weather, the blossom that had appeared on the town's acacias. Then the various family members made excuses and departed one by one, leaving Gyula and Boeske alone. Neither was naïve; neither was lacking in self-confidence. As a child, I liked to hear my mother's version of this meeting.

Boeske asked the young man to remove his hat; she wanted to see the colour of his hair. By that time Gyula's hair was already receding. They both laughed and the ice was broken. A little more conversation, more smiles – all very polite but with a developing intimacy. They liked each other. Each had a sense of humour, each knew how to laugh, each found the other attractive, and they shared a sense of a flourishing future. If it were up to them, they would marry.

But it wasn't up to them – not entirely. Gyula must formally ask Ignac Kellner for his daughter's hand. And so, on another day not long after, Gyula, in his suit and polished shoes and with his freshly brushed homburg hat, again knocked on the door of the Kellner house and asked to speak with the head of the family. Both men again met in the study, uttered Hebrew phrases of greeting and seated themselves comfortably. Tea was served.

It was Ignac Kellner who spoke first – in Hungarian now. 'And your business, young man?'

'Sir, I am here to speak about your eldest daughter.'

'I am waiting.'

'Sir, your daughter Boeske – I would like to marry her.'

Ignac saw attractive qualities in the young man who was asking for his daughter's hand, but he didn't give his final approval right then and there. He had a few reservations. All the enquiries he had made about this prospective son-in-law's character added up to a rousing endorsement: he was a devoted son to his parents; he was kind; he had a good heart; he was honest; he ran a sound business. But Ignac would have been better pleased, for example, if Gyula had been more fully versed in scripture, more knowledgeable about the lessons of the Torah, better able to quote and argue the questions posed in the Talmud. But not every young man had the opportunity and means to grapple with the nuances of the Talmud's thousand authors. Ignac promised the young man that he would give the proposal serious thought. He would go north to Kassa and talk to the sages of his family, and of his wife's family.

It was the custom of Jews to enter into a broad consultation on such matters as this – to bring some sort of tribal wisdom to bear. All manner of opinions might be expressed: Torah might be quoted, or someone with learning might reach into the Talmud and quote the words of a rabbi of ages past – of Ben Zoma from the second century, of Rabbi Hillel, whose thought was so subtle, maybe of Rebbe Nachman of Bratislava, much closer to home.

Ignatiz went to Kassa, and the discussions led to a simple question: 'Is he a good man, this Gyula the cattle dealer?'

'He is a good man,' Ignac replied.

'And Boeske, does she like him?'

'Boeske says she likes him.'

'Then we surely have an answer. He is a good man, Boeske likes him, they will prosper.'

Gyula Keimovits and Boeske Kellner at their engagement, 1922.

Ignac returned to Nyírbátor, called for Boeske and told her that she was free to marry Gyula. He conveyed a message to Gyula, asking him to call at the house. And when he arrived, Ignac said: 'Gyula, I gladly take you to be my son-in-law.'

'Mr Kellner, I thank you with all my heart,' was Gyula's answer.

'There is one condition,' said Ignac. 'You are not to take my daughter to America. I know you have six siblings there. Promise me you won't take my daughter away.'

And Gyula, my father, gave his promise.

Gyula and Boeske were wed on the twenty-seventh day of April, 1922. Gyula was twenty-six, Boeske was twenty-two – the ideal variation in age. Boeske was in the full bloom of her beauty; Gyula was still young but had a well-established business. It was a joyous wedding. All those present could see the deep delight of the new husband and wife. Gyula placed the ring on Boeske's finger and made the wedding declaration: 'Behold, with this ring you are consecrated to me, according to the law of Moses of Israel.' The *ketubah* was signed.

The rabbi offered his seven blessings. As is the custom, the groom broke the glass underfoot; those present cried out: '*Mazel tov!*'

My mother and father's married life began in this patch of eastern Hungary, and it was, as foreseen, a flourishing marriage. April was the marriage month; the following January, with no time wasted, the first of Gyula and Boeske's three children was born.

My sister Erna brought both joy and grief, for she came into

9

Ignac Kellner and Carolina Kellner (née Goldstein).
Carolina was Ignac's second wife. His first wife was her sister Margit
(Boeske's mother), who died while giving birth to Boeske's sister, Marta.

the world with a dislocated hip that required a great deal of attention before it was repaired. I came next, almost five years later, a longer span between first child and second than my mother desired. She thought there was something wrong with her, since Erna had come so quickly, and finally resorted to the spa waters of Hévíz, in the far west of Hungary, with its famous thermal lake. It was said that the Hévíz waters could not only cure infirmities, they could also hasten pregnancies. The waters did the trick, and nine months later there I was, healthy and happy and adored by my parents. Fifteen months later, Marta was born. The family would grow no larger.

The Keimovits family, about 1909. This is probably Gyula's bar mitzvah family photo. He stands middle front, proudly displaying the chain of his bar mitzvah watch. His parents, Rudolf and Gisella (née Grunfeld), stand at the rear with their eldest son, Jeno. In front, from left, are Imre, Henry, Gyula, Mendel and Margit. Missing from the photo are Relli (Rose), the eldest daughter, who had already migrated to the United States, and Joseph, who was about nineteen at this time and was in the military. Gisella bore sixteen children; nine died in childbirth or soon after. Both Rudolf and Gisella died in the 1920s during a typhoid epidemic. All the others except Gyula migrated to America that same decade.

CHAPTER 2

The Beginning

I was born on the fifteenth of December, 1927, at home, with the aid of a midwife – the custom in those times. According to my mother, I was a happy baby, always ready to smile. Visitors to our house in Pócsi Utca never heard a whimper from me. New faces didn't alarm me, and the gooing sounds that adults make when a new baby is displayed to them must have sounded like music to my tiny ears. My unmarried uncle, Bimi, came all the way from Budapest to see the family when I was three months old, and after a stay of a few days said to my proud mother: 'Boeske, can this baby cry? I have never heard her cry, not once.'

It is my theory that a woman who is happy throughout her pregnancy brings into the world a happy baby. My mother spent the whole period of my pregnancy in a state of delighted excitement. By this time, the harrowing problems that had followed the birth of Erna had been resolved, and my mother was able to

Here Erna is at the age of about eleven. In front of her are Baba (on the left), aged about five, and Marta, about four.

give herself with a full heart to the birth of a second child. (In further support of my theory, I must say that I was immensely happy throughout each of my own three pregnancies, and my three sons were all cheerful, thriving babies.)

My birth was a joy to my mother and to my father, as I say. But within a few days the joy vanished: my mother's life was in danger. She had fallen victim to what was known then as 'childbirth fever'; more correctly, it is puerperal fever, an infection caused by the use of unsterilised instruments during delivery, or perhaps by the midwife not having washed her hands well enough. My mother was rushed to a hospital in Debrecen, a city forty kilometres south-west of Nyírbátor, where she hovered between life and death for many days, returning home only after six long weeks.

In a maternity ward of the present day, the fever that threatened my mother's life would have been overcome quickly with antibiotics. But it was less certain in 1927. In my mother's mind during her brief moments of lucidity at the Debrecen hospital would have been the experience of her own mother, who died of this same fever. My father, so I was told much later, found it almost impossible to look at me in my cradle. Instead of gazing down lovingly at his newborn daughter, as he had when I was first delivered, he saw a fiend who had almost cost him his beautiful young wife. But he recovered and became the adoring father of my memories.

Boeske might have waited three or four years before becoming pregnant again, considering what she'd endured. But no. She was pregnant once more within six months. Marta, my youngest sister, was born on the twenty-ninth of March, 1929. And she was an angry child who cried incessantly. Doesn't Marta confirm my theory of happy babies produced by blissful pregnancies? Because my mother's third pregnancy was not blissful. Her memories of the pain and sickness that came so close to ending her life after my birth were still vivid.

My little sister was born on a Friday night. On the morning of the following day, Shabbat, my father went to his father-in-law's house to deliver the good news. 'The child was born last night, and it is a healthy child, and Boeske is well.' My mother's family didn't enquire as to the gender of the baby. They knew it was a girl – or should I say, another girl. Had the new baby been a boy, Gyula would have hurried to the house in the middle of the night wearing a huge smile and shouting proudly: 'I have a son! A son has been born to us!'

We of the Keimovits family had been reasonably well off, but these were the days of the Great Depression and things were tough. Everything was simple, plain and ordinary. Loving parents, games to play, stories read to us. Oh, the stories. Of all the enjoyments my childhood provided, I am especially grateful that books and reading were amongst them.

I can't say when my love for books began; at three years, four, five? The magic of the tales and rhymes would have been enhanced by the cadence of my mother's voice. At maybe four or five, I began to read the stories myself. Throughout my life, in times of distress, I have taken consolation in reading. It has been an ever-present passion, truly. With years it has grown, and it has never abated. My house today is full of books, shelves reaching from the floor to the ceiling. I will sometimes catch the title on the spine of a book and find myself overcome by the rapture of recalling exactly when I first read it, in what circumstances, and I will take down the book and forget all my duties.

As Erna was five years older than me, naturally she was a little remote. I might have asked her to read me a story when my mother was busy, but we didn't play together much. It was my younger sister, Marta, who was my playmate – I hovered over her like a second mother.

My concern for her wellbeing approached paranoia on occasions. Like most houses in rural Hungary, ours had a lavatory at the far end of our backyard; there was no sewerage system, and people naturally wanted to keep the smell as far from the house as possible. The big timber seat comfortably accommodated adults, but it was too large for little bodies, unless they were alert to the danger. I remember vividly my fear that Marta would fall through the hole to certain death, and I followed her down to the lavatory every time she required a visit. I was like a ministering angel – in this case, the ministering angel of the lavatory.

The fretting Marta caused me went further. I had very little understanding of death beyond the obvious: that when a person was dead, he or she ceased to move or talk, and very soon disappeared entirely. I once overheard someone say, 'After he died, I

Marta at kindergarten in Nyírbátor; she is the second child from the right.

closed his eyes,' and I was clever enough to draw the conclusion that a person could be dead with eyes wide open. Marta, like many other small children, was capable of sleeping or drowsing with her eyes half open. I would stare down at her as she slept, her eyelids fluttering, and when the thought that my little sister was close to death became too much to bear, I would gently wake her to make sure she was still alive. In years to come, I would learn much more about death, but I never feared anyone's death with quite the intensity that dwelt in me when I sat beside Marta's cot.

Whether in winter's snow or the clear air of summer, the day in Nyírbátor began for Erna and Marta and me when the sound of the hooter from the Bohny bread factory blared rudely at seven in the morning. Bohny was Nyírbátor's sole manufacturing plant, and the hooter signalled the start of the working day. All I ever knew about Bohny was that it produced this bread, which we purchased fresh for our table every morning. I think the plant also included a distillery. The manager of the plant was Mr Zeger, an assimilated Jew, high on the social ladder of Nyírbátor. His beautiful blonde daughter, Annushka, was a friend of Marta's.

The best time to be carefree is during childhood, when the world is fresh and vivid – when a game played in the street with your friends, or a sunset, or the flight of birds across the sky, or an ice-cream at the cake shop in the town square thrills and delights you. I recall long spring evenings playing catch on the street, running between the acacia trees with other children of the neighbourhood, all of them my friends. If you touched a tree before the others caught you, you won. And other games too: hide-and-seek, or the many variations of skipping – a long rope swung by a playmate standing at each end, me in the middle leaping while rhymes were chanted. The acacias were in full bloom, and their heavy, sweet fragrance mingled with the dust of the unpaved street. We were uninhibited in our happiness.

The only thing that interrupted our play was the ambling return of the cattle from the common grazing fields at sundown. We gave way to the herds and watched in fascination as the ponderous beasts lumbered past. It always seemed a minor miracle to me that each cow and each calf knew where it lived, where it belonged. As first one gate, then another swung open, and each beast chose its own yard without any urging from the peasant herdsmen who followed them. Then came the pigs, the sows and their young – big creatures, the sows. There I stood, a hand to my nose, curious about the pigs despite their smell, noticing the way the younger pigs kept close to their mothers. I was curious about everything as a child, as if the world were an inexhaustible source of the strange, the wonderful and the downright puzzling. The swineherds wore black, round-domed hats, and capes that could be slung to hang down the back or pulled around to cover more of the upper body on cold days. The costume of the swineherds was not the same as that of the cattle herders; there were a few differences in the shape of the hats and capes. I took an interest in such things.

The stench of the pigs never bothered us; we were country children and we never shied away from what was natural in life. We were immersed in nature, in its sounds and smells. Certainly I was a civilised being – I knew my manners, I read books, I learned my lessons at school. But part of me was wild, as if I retained some vital spark of the life people lived before the time of books and schools and learning. That's what it is to be free, I think: to feel thrilled by what one's senses provide, and then to go home to warmth and shelter and open a book. I'm not sure that one can ever again be quite as free as in childhood.

The cows went by, the pigs went by and we resumed our games. We wanted to go on playing, running and laughing forever. Every evening, when I heard my mother's voice calling us home for supper, I felt a moment's sadness. The day was over. The fun must wait for another day.

By nine o'clock I was fed and bathed and in my bed. And nine o'clock was also the hour that the soldiers stationed in Nyírbátor were called to their barracks by a mournful bugle. The sound roused the dogs of the neighbourhood to a frenzy, as if they considered it their duty to make a din louder than the bugler's. The notes of the instrument combined with the racket of the barking dogs always touched off a fear in me, as if the world outside my bedroom had taken on a darker mood. Then an immense sadness settled on my heart. Where did it come from? Was it a warning of some sort, that the world had more to show me than games and sunsets and the interesting spectacle of cows and pigs returning home in the dusk?

I whispered my Hebrew prayers, repeating the last verse until I had lulled myself to sleep. The following morning, before the hooter at the factory sounded, I would be briefly awakened by the notes of different bugles: the herdsmen and swineherds calling their beasts back out to pasture. Each played a different three or four notes. I would listen in my drowsy state, then ask myself: 'Baba, did you finish your prayers last night?'

I'd fall asleep again until the Bohny hooter sounded. By then all thoughts of sadness had vanished. I thought only of fresh bread, of the morning greeting from my mother, and of the fun that the new day would bring.

In front of the Keimovits family house at 1 Pócsi Utca in about 1934.
Gyula and Boeske stand at the right, and Boeske's half-sister Manci at the left.
Hedy Hammerman sits at the far left, then Marta, Erna and Baba.

CHAPTER 3

Shabbat

It has been said that women lose their sense of play once they become mothers; that the responsibilities of parenting place them at greater and greater distance from the spirit of the games they once enjoyed. That wasn't true of my mother. She retained her feeling for play even when she was caring for three children and a husband. It was a part of her essence.

She played shops and housewives and kindergarten with Marta and me, also with Erna when she was younger. She had to be in a good mood, of course, but she was often in a good mood. She entered into the games not with the patient forbearance of an adult, but with the glee of a child. It may even have been a release for her, to caper in the way she did. When my father returned home from his work, my mother stepped straight back into her adult role as wife, and whatever game we were engaged in was over. I resented my father's intrusion, and wished he'd been delayed.

It was not only the games my mother played with me and Marta and the books she read to us that thrilled me – she also sang to us. She loved to sing. Her voice was warm and lyrical, and she sang from the heart. Marta and I, and often Erna too, sat around her while she entertained us, our gazes on her face, drawn in by the enchantment of her voice. And she knew so many songs: Hungarian folk songs, others that she recalled from the musicals of her younger years, some from light opera. Just as the games she played with us gave her pleasure, so the singing enriched her days. Can one sing like that, with such tenderness and expression, without enjoying oneself?

How I loved the sentimental songs fashionable during the First World War! It's so strange to think that the early twentieth century, such a catastrophic period, should have produced an abundance of songs that spoke of love and home and hearth, of sunshine and blossom, of the devotion of a mother or a father, or of the loyalty of a sweetheart. Or perhaps it's not strange that such songs became popular when men were fighting each other in the mud.

There were comic songs, too, even one or two with a satirical edge. I picked up all these tunes from my mother, and I know them still, all these decades later. I begin to hum a tune, and almost instantly the words return and out they tumble, all in Hungarian, my native tongue. I may not have thought of the song for years, but I've retained every syllable of the lyrics, every note of the tune.

Our Jewishness braced our lives in the way that a trellis supports the vine that is woven through it. But neither I nor my sisters, nor even our parents, gave much thought to our Jewishness. We were not self-conscious about our faith. It was a natural part of our lives. I don't believe I ever once compared, in an objective way, what happened in our household with what went on in Christian households. We followed our own customs, and nothing else needed to be said.

An observant Jew has a great many rules to honour. Dietary observances account for hundreds; they influence everything you eat. Only observant Jews know the pitfalls of eating away from a kosher table. Yet we did not labour under a heavy burden of observance. It came to us without any anguished reflection: my mother prepared kosher, we ate kosher, and that was all there was to it. Of course we rigorously kept Shabbat and all the Jewish festivals.

On those days no work is allowed; even making a fire or turning on a light is considered physical labour. When Shabbat commenced on a Friday evening, our house seemed to be cleaner, more sparkling, and the atmosphere was warm and welcoming. The table was laid with a crisp white tablecloth, and at the centre of the table stood a candlestick holder with seven candles flickering. These represented my parents and their three children; my mother added one for a sister of hers who died as a young woman, and for their mother, who died at the age of twenty-two. The candlelight spread a tender radiance on our household.

Before the sun sets, marking the beginning of Shabbat, it is the duty of the mistress of the house to light the candles of the Shabbat ceremony, and to say a blessing as the flame rises from each wick. Every time I light the candles now, I recall how my father found a way to play his part in the ceremony. He lit each candle for a few seconds, then snuffed it out, so that when the time came for my mother to light the candles, the shorter wick would yield an instantaneous flame.

After the prayer which welcomed the arrival of Queen Shabbat, my father filled a goblet with red wine, in preparation for the recital of the *kiddush*. Shabbat is always known as the 'queen' or the 'bride', a tradition going back so long that no story of its origin properly explains it. It's not something that we dwelt on; we all rose from our seats at the table as my father lifted the goblet, welcomed Queen Shabbat and blessed the wine. The goblet went around the table and each of us took a sip.

Father would then lift the cloth cover from the *challah* and offer a prayer. He cut generous slices and handed one to Mother, then to Erna, to me, to Marta, to all who were seated at our table that evening. How delicious that *challah* tasted, not only for itself but also because of the comforting ritual of its serving. Everything we ate on Shabbat evening had the superadded quality of taste imparted by these honoured rituals. It was as if we had been invited to enjoy the first food ever consumed on earth, and so our appreciation was at its keenest.

The whole of the meal was punctuated by songs of praise for

Shabbat. And when the meal was over, we sang, at the top of our voices, a final prayer of gratitude, the *Birkat Hamazon*. For the remainder of Shabbat evening, we relaxed. It was possible to relax on any other day of the week, of course, but this was different – this was relaxation that reached deep down and nourished one's soul.

And Shabbat evening, of course, was only the beginning of twenty-five hours of strict observance – strict, yes, but warmly embraced. When we rose from bed the next morning, we were still enjoying this atmosphere, right up until the evening. It was not a matter of finding things to do that fell within the boundaries of Shabbat; it was an easeful day of conversation and communion. We enjoyed a number of meals (all prepared in advance), and each meal was introduced by prayers and chanting.

If I sit quietly, I can transport myself back to the Keimovits' household just as the sun is setting. Dusk creeps into the room where we women – well, women and girls – sit around the fireplace, while Father sits alone at the table singing King David's twenty-third Psalm. It has a beautiful, mournful melody, and Father sings the psalm three times. We do not join him on these occasions. We just sit quietly, each of us with her own thoughts. All is peaceful and we are content.

Each week there was Shabbat, but only once a year was Pesach, or Passover. Our preparations for Pesach were painstaking. The house was cleaned from top to bottom, and our everyday crockery and cutlery were changed for those that were designated for this special season. I remember feeling a thrill when I saw these bowls and cups and utensils which I hadn't seen for a year. And when Father arrived with the freshly baked *matzah* – big, round, handmade unleavened bread, crisp and thin – I produced another smile. I loved the Seder nights we spent reading the Haggadah, which seemed to grow shorter year by year as I grew older. And my mother was inspired to sing, as if the season of Pesach and its importance called for the contribution of her beautiful voice. She sang not only for her own pleasure and for ours, but to impress on us the words and melodies of the venerable traditions of the Jewish community. I still sing my mother's songs to my own children at the Seder table.

Our neighbourhood in Nyírbátor meant almost as much to me as our dining room, or my own bedroom. The road was wide in front of our house, because at that point it became two streets, Pócsi Utca and Debreceni Utca. Opposite our window was an artesian well, the water raised by a big revolving iron wheel. The handle attached to the wheel had been burnished to a bright silver by the many hands that had grasped it over the years. The most common type of well in Nyírbátor was the backyard draw well: a pail on a rope that was dropped into the reservoir of water below, then drawn up, full, to the surface. But the water of these draw wells was usually too rich in minerals to be used for drinking or cooking. The water of the artesian well, coming from deeper down, was what we relied on for drinking and for bathing. Our bathtub was wooden, made from a hollowed-out tree trunk. My mother would pour heated water from the artesian well into the wooden tub, and we would stand in it and wash, first our upper bodies, then our lower.

It was no great burden for us to take water from the well to our home. Others endured a longer trek. Marta and I, and sometimes Erna too, watched from the window as the people of the neighbourhood visited the well with buckets, some from a long distance away. For them it was a chore each day; even a single bucket of water is heavy, and most families required more than just one.

Anything that happened in our neighbourhood was interesting, sometimes even fascinating. It was not so much to do with gossip, but rather that we were watching the day-to-day lives and stories of people we knew well unfolding before our eyes – the narrative of our town. We noticed if a girl had a new dress, or new shoes, or if someone seemed a little bit ill, or very ill, or more cheerful than usual. Our neighbours were characters in the tale of the town, just as we were to them.

The winters of Nyírbátor made filling buckets a particular trial. The temperature dropped, snow fell, and the water droplets that ran from the fountain of the well froze as the cold air hit them, creating a long icicle. People would break off the icicle before turning the handle on the wheel. And the handle itself would be freezing cold. I never tested it, but I imagine that the flesh of a bare hand could have been fused to the metal. I suppose you can get used to all kinds of hardships.

I have spoken of Jewish ritual and custom in the Keimovits family without making it clear that we lived amongst the non-Jewish people of Nyírbátor – which was to say, the majority – and not in a ghetto of the sort that existed in other parts of Europe. The Jews of Nyírbátor had never been compelled to isolate themselves in a designated area. We lived in the best streets of the town, and in the poorest ones, and whether we were well-to-do or penniless, we all thought of ourselves as Hungarians.

I suppose living with neighbours of one's faith to the left and right reinforces the bond of shared belief. But our family honoured the rituals of our faith without any great fuss. We didn't feel insecure – at least, not in the early 1930s – and we didn't feel the need to live cheek by jowl with other Jews. No Jewish children at all lived close to our house in Pócsi Utca; until I started school, all of my friends were non-Jewish. It's possible those kids I played with on the street knew I was Jewish since I didn't join them on Shabbat, but maybe not. We delighted each other – that was all we cared about.

We had four immediate neighbours in Pócsi Utca. On one side, behind a high wooden fence, lived a middle-aged woman who kept herself so much to herself that she could have been considered a hermit. It was rumoured that she had a husband somewhere, maybe in jail. Nobody knew why, or even if it was true. We were curious, of course, but too well mannered to even think of approaching the lady and asking her. She kept a dog, a real ruffian of a beast, ugly as sin, with a square face that seemed to be designed to repel any attempt at affection. The hermit lady never left her house without this forbidding creature, and it may have been the dog's task to keep us all at a distance. She never spoke a word to anybody in the neighbourhood.

A Jewish family lived over another fence: the Roths. The men of the family had become tailors, while the grown-up girls were all seamstresses. The work of the Roth family seamstresses was mostly alterations; they were not geniuses of the needle and thread. We children liked to go over to the Roths' house because the girls, the seamstresses, allowed us to undo seams. We would pick away at those seams as if we were being granted some wonderful privilege.

The room in which both the tailors and the seamstresses sat working at their machines was long and had a low ceiling, somewhat like a factory. I loved this big workroom: there was such a feeling of industry, of busyness, that I couldn't help but feel excited. The girls were young, but not so young that they couldn't marry, if they wished, yet most were spinsters. Acceptable husbands were in short supply at this time; many young Jewish men had been amongst the hundreds of thousands of Hungarians killed while serving the Emperor during the Great War. Sometimes the Roth girls took us into their small bedrooms. There were two beds per room, with dainty white lace everywhere, and on each bed a fancy doll dressed in pink frills. These bedrooms were so tiny that one might think the dolls were the actual occupants.

On Friday nights the machines were covered, the half-finished works went into cupboards, the floor was swept and the work-room became a small prayer house for the Jews of the neighbourhood and a little further distant. On Saturday morning everybody wanted to go to the big *shul*, but on Friday nights many people were too tired to rouse themselves to attend. They would make a short appearance at the prayer house, then go home, eat dinner and rest. After six days' work, and at a time when a working day for many people lasted twelve hours, that was understandable. My father was often amongst those who availed themselves of this convenient local house of worship.

Behind us lived Iri and Mari, identical twins of my age who had long, straight blonde hair. We were playmates but not really friends. We didn't refer to them by their individual names but with the compound name of IriMari, and they were content to be addressed in that way. IriMari's father was not on the scene. It was quite possible that he never had been, or perhaps no more than once. IriMari's mother was, as you might expect, very poor. She made her living, such as it was, by mending, laundering and ironing. But the girls were our playmates, and that was all we cared about. We never went into their house and they never came into ours.

The Szucs children were in a different category. The two Szucs girls, Anna and Marika, and their older brother, Feri, were very close to the respective ages of the three Keimovits girls, and our friendship with them was perfectly harmonised. We adored them; they adored us. Such intensity in the friendships of childhood! And at the same time a simplicity that we are unlikely ever to experience in our adult years.

The Szucs family was Christian. Come December, for Feri, Anna and Marika, there was a Christmas tree, carols, Christmas dinner, special dishes, presents. And for us there was Hanukkah. I don't think the differences between the two festivals ever had to be exhaustively explained; it was accepted that the Keimovits children did one thing, and the Szucs did another. No big deal, as they say.

Mr Szucs ran a chimney-sweeping business, and made a good living from it. And although we never saw the interior of IriMari's house, we saw the inside of the Szucs children's house all the time. It was a treat to visit. The Szucs home was modern, with a loft that had small, round windows and a floor covered in golden sand. The purpose of the sand was to act as insulation, I imagine, but it meant more than that to me. The smell of it thrilled me, evoking images of beaches and an ocean that I had never actually seen. The loft was an adventure playground of sorts – no obstacles to climb or crawl through, but the sand excited in me a feeling of otherness, of an attractive strangeness, as if I were travelling to another land, like the exotic destinations in the books I read with such relish. The round windows were like the portholes of a ship, and although I had never seen a ship, it was easy to imagine that the loft was a proud vessel riding the swell of the ocean.

Holidaying at the thermal baths of Hajdúszoboszló.
Cousin Kati Lichtman from Budapest is at the left, with Erna and Marta on the right.
Sitting is Baba, not wearing a bathing costume due to a cold.

We never came to the end of our enjoyment of that loft. We brought toys with us, including our dolls, as if this special place had to be shared with those toys for which we had such love. The Szucs loft was, in fact, a separate home for us, one we had fashioned ourselves, where our passions and priorities ruled, and where our lives were at their most vivid. When I picture the Szucs house, I think of a drawing by Erna. She once chose to depict the house for a school assignment. The genius of Erna's draughting was celebrated in our family, and her drawing of the Szucs house was a masterpiece, perfect in every detail. We said, 'Erna, how are you able to do that?' It really was something. Even when I gaze at it now, in my mind's eye, it seems to me better than a photograph.

Each year our family enjoyed a holiday away from Nyírbátor, often to the spa at Hajdúszoboszló. A special delight was to return with presents for Feri, Anna and Marika, knowing that they would also have presents for us. The Szucs family always went to the home of the children's grandparents, Szerencs, in the north of Hungary, a town only half the size of Nyírbátor but which boasted the biggest sugar refinery in Europe. Szerencs was famous above all for its chocolate. We could always anticipate the treat of chocolates, the perfect gift, when we met up with the Szucs kids after our holidays.

I've seen enough in my life, and read enough of the experience of others to know that friendships between Jews and gentiles, particularly at this point of the twentieth century, often frayed. The Nazis were a robust political force in Germany, and even without their propaganda, Hungary was a nation historically susceptible to outbreaks of anti-Semitism. There was plenty of it about in Nyírbátor and its region at a time when I was old enough to know what it meant.

A few years later than this, troops of Hungarian soldiers marched through the town, singing loudly:

Hey, Jew, hey, Jew, hey, you stinking Jew
What are you doing here amongst us Hungarians?
Under your side-locks lice are crawling
Your mother Zali was smuggled into our land
In a sack on your father's back

And:

Because the Jew is of a kosher kind
It feels so good to hit him hard.

The prejudice that informed these grotesque sentiments remained dormant for a time, only to be stirred up by virulent slogans and broadcasts. How happy I am to say that in those days the Szucs family never gave the slightest indication of sympathy with such anti-Semitic rants.

The loving friendship between the Szucs children and us remained unsullied until one day in 1938 when we saw Feri in the street. As we walked past him, he looked at us and hissed, 'Stinking Jews!'

In front of the Keimovits home at 1 Pócsi Utca in about 1936; the Greek Orthodox church is visible in the background. The family was farewelling the Hammermans, who were leaving for Palestine.
Margit Hammerman (Boeske's half-sister) is in the top centre. Hedy, her daughter, is on the far right. Between them is Boeske. Erna stands on the far left, and Manci, another of Boeske's half-sisters, is next to her. In front of them are Marta (left) and Baba.

CHAPTER 4

Learning

Between roughly 1932, when I was five, and 1934, when I was seven, Marta and I attended kindergarten, just across the way from our front door in Pócsi Utca. The kindergarten welcomed kids of all social classes. We counted in our number the children of a policeman, of shopkeepers, even of a local Lutheran preacher. And some who, judging by their dress, came from peasant families.

It was still a time when you could be a Jew in Nyírbátor in an unselfconscious way, but in kindergarten the dominant faith of the town, Christianity, took precedence. When mid-December came around, the Christmas nativity play attracted devoted attention from the teachers and the kids. We Jewish children never took an active part in the Christmas play. We sat through the rehearsals, not entirely without interest, learnt the songs and the hymns, but we were not participants. The teachers and the

Christian kids certainly didn't scorn us, but it was evident that we were outsiders. I didn't protest, but Christmas in kindergarten gave me an incipient understanding of what it might mean to dwell in the margins of a community. It wasn't tragic, just strange. For those few days in December, the Jewish children of the kinder withdrew into a type of limbo.

But I was still watching and noticing. I remember clearly one Christmas play in which the role of baby Jesus was given to an unkempt little girl with tangled fair hair. She looked inadequately nourished, and spent the whole of each rehearsal in a basket. She had no lines to utter, and she gazed about, baffled, one hand tucked between her thighs. None of the other kids in the rather large cast – the Magi, shepherds, angels – paid any attention to what baby Jesus was up to, and the teacher appeared oblivious. Even baby Jesus herself seemed unaware.

Our kindergarten teacher was a plump, not so gentle old maid in her late fifties. She lived on the premises with her diminutive mother. This ancient lady sat throughout the day in an armchair in the middle of the room in which we children sang and played. She remained almost motionless for the whole time we were there, bundled up in a colourful crocheted rug. She slept at times – well, her eyes were closed – but for the most part she simply stared straight ahead, at nothing.

Anger always seemed to be brewing in our teacher, who was assisted by a sturdy peasant maid. One of the maid's winter tasks was to keep the fire burning in our room throughout the day, adding coals to the glowing embers. One winter's day we were indoors, as was usual when the playground was covered in snow. The fire was glowing, the ancient lady was sleeping under her crocheted rug, and we children were playing quietly in scattered groups. I happened to be in a group close to our teacher when she suddenly felt the need to chastise a girl in another group. 'You rude little runt, how dare you use such filthy language?' she roared. 'I will burn out your tongue!'

I was startled. The phrase 'burn out your tongue' arrested me, and I glimpsed the maid shuffling toward the fire. She picked up the poker and jabbed the tip into the glowing embers, leaving it there to grow red-hot. I thought: 'The poker is being prepared to burn out that girl's tongue, and I will be forced to watch.' A surge of panic rose into my chest, and I fainted there, where I sat.

This swoon in the kindergarten was my first, but it would not be my last. For years after, whenever I faced sudden physical, psychological or emotional rigour that came without warning, my brain short-circuited. These lapses into unconsciousness were not unwelcome. Escape from the immediate was one benefit, but there was another, for as soon as I fainted, I began to dream, and the dreams were always enjoyable, even rhapsodic.

When I regained consciousness, the teacher and the maid were bent over me with concerned expressions. But I was fine. I remembered the rapture I'd just experienced and had no fear of it returning at some future time. I hadn't hurt myself by

Marta, Erna and Baba in the yard of their house at 1 Pócsi Utca.

collapsing – indeed, in all my future syncopic episodes, I never suffered bruises, abrasions, fractures.

I recall clearly one Thursday morning in September 1934: I was preparing for my first day of school in Nyírbátor. Marta was still attending kindergarten, but here I was, at age six, about to commence a new stage of my education. Erna was of course already a schoolgirl, and for some time I had envied her. On that first morning, I was so wildly excited that I couldn't manage to put my own clothes on, and my mother had to help me. I babbled on in a torrent of delight, even going so far as to tell my elder sister: 'Erna, you will no longer have to read me stories, for after today I will be able to read everything myself.'

Erna laughed at me. 'No, not after one day, Baba, it will take longer than that.'

I was annoyed – how dare she! 'I will be reading as soon as I come home!' I said. 'You'll see!'

While I started out with unrealistic ideas about learning, I was indeed reading a few months after commencing school. My enthusiasm for school was not only for the increased opportunities for play or the chance to make new friends, but for learning itself.

I recall a day almost a year before that first day at school. I was in the kitchen of our house with my mother and Marta. I was sitting at the low children's table we kept in the kitchen, and Marta was on another chair. Our mother was busy preparing dinner, carrying a big, black pot from the table to the stove. I had a book of poems open before me on the table, a book from which my mother often read aloud. I was leaning over the book and reciting a poem to my sister – but the poem I was reciting was not in the book. I was making it up as I went along, imitating what my mother did when she read aloud to us: keeping my eyes on the lines before me, turning the pages at intervals with a wetted fingertip. The poem was not gibberish; it had fluency, meaning, rhyme and rhythm. As soon as I came to the end of the poem – and I somehow knew when I reached the end – the words, the lines, vanished from my memory. I was overwhelmed by my talent and tears ran down my cheeks. My sister stared at me wide-eyed.

That first school I attended was a Jewish day school, which offered Nyírbátor's Jewish community a curriculum spread over six compulsory grades. As happens amongst children, the pre-school friendships I thought would last for eternity began to fade away as new friendships developed. The schoolhouse was less than a kilometre from our home in Pócsi Utca, a ten-minute walk away. The headmaster and his wife lived there, and there were three rooms for the kids and a tiny apartment for a janitor. The headmaster was about fifty, with a strong build and a broad face that remained as red as a tomato all day. He was a pompous man, full of self-importance, as if he'd been granted his office and authority by the king himself. His wife was a colourless creature; the only thing I remember about her was her size. The fat wife and the red-faced husband had no children.

Classes started at eight o'clock in the morning, which in winter meant that Erna and I headed off to school half an hour after sunrise. The pale light reflecting off the snow lent an element of mystery to the journey. In spring, the birds sang a chorus of encouragement. In summer we would sometimes see storks and wild ducks. I had a leather bag slung over my shoulder, a few books inside and also my lunch: buttered bread wrapped in greaseproof paper, and a piece of fruit. I chattered away inside my head as I walked, noticing everything, asking myself questions. Some of the thoughts that engaged me had a philosophical aspect. One morning it occurred to me that animals, even insects, might have souls. In the newspaper death notices, the announcement always noted that a person 'exhaled his or her noble soul'. What did a flea exhale at its death? The question perplexed me. I raised it at school amongst my friends and was surprised that they had no interest. They thought I was crazy.

Our school had two sessions each day. In the morning, the three lower grades occupied the schoolhouse. At half-past twelve this first group of students departed for home; the place was spruced up by the janitor, and at one o'clock the higher three grades came to study. The facilities were somewhat spartan. We wrote in pencil until third grade, when we were judged mature enough to use ink. There was only a tiny open space outdoors for play, and not much more room indoors, for that matter. But the tuition was thorough, taking in maths, history and geography, and we kids loved the school and respected the education it provided. It was *our* school. We were given a cup of warm milk at second playtime, and were grateful for it. For some kids from poorer families, this may have been their most sustaining nourishment of the day. Sometimes, in the winter, the janitor would bring us freshly baked squares of pumpkin.

Néni is a Hungarian word usually translated as 'auntie'. It was the semi-official title of our teachers at the Jewish school. *Néni* really means 'a woman who has the authority to act in the role of a close relative, but with more firmness than one would normally expect to be exercised by an actual aunt'. Marishka Néni was my teacher for first and second grades, and I adored her. She was around thirty, unmarried, and devoted to the kids in her class. Like most teachers, she had her favourites amongst the children, and I was pleased that I was one. My eagerness to learn, and my ability, commended me to her. My small transgressions were of the sort that teachers of Marishka Néni's sort find forgivable. She would often discover me reading a book under the desk; her remonstrations were mild.

Idushka Néni was my third-grade teacher, and I knew even before I stepped into her classroom in 1936 that she was stricter than her colleague, and less inclined to overlook my penchant for reading during class. On my first day in her class, at the age of nine, I listened attentively and restrained my compulsion to read my book under the desk – for that day at least. As it turned out, I had nothing to worry about. Certainly Idushka Néni was tougher than Marishka Néni, but she was no monster.

When school was over for the day, I walked to a shop nearby owned by my uncle and waited there for my mother. I'd chatter cheerfully with my uncle, then chatter just as cheerfully with my mother as we walked home. I could go from waking in the morning to falling asleep at night with barely a frown to crease my brow.

I see now that my childhood in Nyírbátor prepared my sisters and me for a passionate engagement with life. Loving parents, a certain level of material comfort, conscientious schooling. The moral dimension of our lives, nourished by our parents, was equally straightforward. We were expected to be courteous, kind, generous. We did not mock those less fortunate than we were.

The project of building a good life – of raising happy children, of running a modest household, of making an income that will feed and clothe a family – is not a superhuman undertaking. It is, I think, a natural way to go about things. And there need only be a small complement of goodness in any person to turn him away from the evil things he might imagine. An alternative existed for Feri Szucs when he shouted out his foolish slogan. That alternative was to recall that we had once played together happily. For Feri Szucs, every Feri Szucs, this is an alternative of far greater reward.

CHAPTER 5

The May Beetles

Laws that discriminated against Jews had already been enacted by 1937. No Jewish student was permitted to attend any Hungarian university, for instance. This meant that Erna, Marta and I would have to go elsewhere if we wanted a university education. But I didn't think of universities in 1937. I thought of the Jewish day school, where I had reached the fourth grade. I thought, too, of our headmaster, Mr Gondosh, and my thoughts were not endearing.

He was not a Jew who took comfort from belonging to the Jewish community of Nyírbátor, but instead identified with the much broader Hungarian gentile community. He had changed his name from Gottlieb, a common Jewish surname, to the solidly Hungarian name of Gondosh. He was a loyal supporter of the Hungarian monarchy and wished his allegiance to be as conspicuous as possible. He required his students to stand and come to attention whenever the name of the Hungarian Regent, Horthy

Miklós, was mentioned. It was mentioned often. Once we'd leapt
to attention, we raised our chins and recited a formal commen-
dation, like vassals: 'Long live Horthy Miklós, His Majesty, Regent
of Hungary.' We couldn't have cared less about the Regent and
were embarrassed by this stupid and gratuitous charade; we knew
nonsense when we heard it.

One of my classmates was a boy named Sanyi. He had a ruddy,
round face. The son of a landholder, he came from a little village
outside of Nyírbátor. (I learned only later that Sanyi was a cousin
of the man who would become my husband.) Sanyi was a happy
kid, always smiling. Gondosh made him sit in the first row so
that he would be nearby whenever Gondosh took it into his head
to slap Sanyi's face. The poor child never did anything to invite
these slaps – Gondosh just didn't like him. Whenever he administered a slap, he called out cruelly: 'Your face invites me for a
slap.' Did he think this was witty? What an extraordinary thing
that we could still adore our little school despite the bullying of
this self-important, detestable Gondosh.

Poor Sanyi was not Gondosh's only victim. His prey included
a number of boys and girls, children he detested for one reason or
another, perhaps because they were strugglers academically. All
were punished without the least explanation.

On the morning of the fifteenth of December, 1937, I mentioned to Mr Gondosh that it was my birthday. It was the custom
in Hungary, when your birthday came around, for your friends,
your schoolmates and your relatives to give you a gentle tug on

your left earlobe as a sign of recognition. The headmaster had me stand in front of his desk while all the kids in the class approached me, one by one, and tugged my earlobe. Thirty-five kids altogether administered the birthday tug, including the very religious class members, boys with long *payot*, who would not normally take part in such a ritual. I walked home from school along the familiar paths with a very sore ear and a sense of having deserved the pain for my vanity.

My birthday presents were waiting for me when I arrived home. Nothing big and gaudy – small things, inexpensive, such as a card game of ingenious design, and another game that called for the player to manipulate an oblong glass case, in which small silver balls rolled. The object of the game was to make the silver balls drop into tiny holes. When you had trapped all the balls in the holes, you had triumphed and could scatter the balls and attempt to triumph all over again.

While I was enjoying myself with my games, I happened to reach up and touch my left earlobe. I discovered that my earring was gone. These earrings of mine were much loved. Five light-blue precious stones making a five-petal flower, with a tiny gold bubble at the centre. I could only think that it had been snatched from my ear by one of my classmates, either accidentally or intentionally. To lose an earring was not a catastrophe, but it is still the first thing that comes to my mind when I think back to 1937.

So I was ten. I had lived a full decade in Nyírbátor, and my life had been crammed with gladness. When in a vague way I contemplated the path ahead of me, the anti-Semites of Hungary and Germany did not make my future seem especially fraught. My mother listened to the news on the radio and read the newspapers. She shared the news with my father, and also with her children. I listened, of course, but not with genuine alarm, or even foreboding. To be honest, my greatest fear at the age of ten was the same as it had been at the age of nine, and eight, and seven, and even further back.

As I have said, my mother was in charge of discipline in our family and was capable of administering slaps and smacks whenever she thought it necessary. I was afraid of her. I dreaded rousing her to anger, or even causing her to be displeased with me. The thought made me feel ill.

My mother's ingenuity I also recall. She had to be ingenious, for in the years following the Great Depression, every family in Hungary (like almost everywhere else) had to make the household budget stretch further. My father's six siblings, who had migrated to America at the start of the century, would send us packages every so often, thinking of us as the strugglers of the family. Of course, they were themselves hit hard by the Depression, but maybe not as hard as we Hungarians. They sent bundles of used clothing, and from the fabric of these garments my mother had dresses made for Erna and Marta and me. The very fact that our dresses had originated in America imparted a glamour that Marta and I acted out by talking loudly to each other in gibberish – our version of the American language.

We played in all manner of ways. What a delight it was to leave footprints in the freshly fallen snow that covered the road on the way to school. I placed one shod foot after another, after another, after another, then I turned my head to see the indentations I had left. It was as if I had left my signature on the snow. With other children, I would run and then slide on the soles of my shoes along a flat surface of snow that had been compressed into an ice sheet. Who could slide the furthest? By this time Jewish children were unwelcome at the frozen artificial pond in Nyírbátor, where the children of the more well-to-do Christian families went to skate. The laws that regulated what Jews could and could not do were not always specific; often it was a matter of assumption. If we could not go here and we could not go there, maybe we could not go skating on the pond. So we didn't go, and because we didn't, it became a de facto ban. It was the same with the tennis court and the public swimming pool.

Jewish exclusion in Nyírbátor at this time was something like being ostracised. But it was much more vicious. It wounded me to be disdained in that way. Even though I was a child, I deplored injustice – and this was clearly an injustice. Jews live every day with a heightened awareness of injustice. It has been a part of Jewish consciousness for centuries. We are born into a legacy of injustice, and it never goes away. At the age of ten, I was forced to endure an injustice that was baffling for its lack of foundation.

A little later than the events I am relating now, a Catholic girl told me, with an expression of malicious triumph, that our Regent

Horthy could never be King Horthy because he wasn't a Catholic; he was a Lutheran. She took pleasure in knowing that Horthy lacked this fine but necessary distinction. I experienced a moment of illumination. I thought: 'Oh, so it is not just Jews who are scorned. The Christian Catholics think the Christian Lutherans, too, are dreadful people!'

By the spring of 1938, the snow had melted. At school we were studying the emergence of the May beetle. It's a large, nut-brown beetle, with double wings and serrated legs. I thought the May beetle beautiful, even though I had a near phobia of insects. Even today, these beetles are the only insects I am willing to touch. They tickle your fingers when you handle them.

The larvae of the May beetle live on the roots of plants and emerge only once every four years. They gather in great numbers on the acacia trees, emitting a strident sound. For some reason, Nyírbátor's schools paid the children of the town to shake the trees, dislodge the May beetles in their thousands, gather them up in cardboard boxes and turn them over to the beetle authority. Inside the boxes – some small, some large – the beetles would crawl over each other in their panic, a seething mass of them, deeply fascinating to watch. The beetles could open their wings and fly away, but they almost never did. It was as if they accepted their captive status: that they would likely never know the freedom of their acacia trees again.

A group photograph of the Saturday afternoon Jewish girls' club, Club Miriam, in 1941. The girls are all aged thirteen or fourteen.

Top row, from left: Lili Galet, Eva Rothberger, Magda Blier, Magda Schwartz, Edi Katz(?), Boeske Roth(?), Kato Weinberger, Anna Berger, Baba Keimovits. Middle row: unknown, Eva Ratz, Marta Keimovits, Mrs Lemberger (Rabbi's wife), Piroska Grunfeld (the group's organiser), Eva Schwartz, Magda Klein (Andor Schwartz's cousin), Ver Fried, Annushka Zeger. Front row: Erna Fetman, Gabi Friedman, Eva Berger.

These names are accurate to the best of Baba's recollection. There is no one left to confirm them with. (If there is a reader of this book who can provide any corrections, please inform the publisher.) Baba is certain that Eva Rothberg, her sister Marta, Piroska Grunfeld, Eva Schwarz, Magda Klein and Anna Berger survived the Holocaust. Annushka Zeger died on the death march, as we will read later.

CHAPTER 6

High School

I took after my mother, Erna took after my father, and Marta was a hybrid, with some of each. There was not a person in the world I would rather have resembled than my mother. But in one regard it would have been better for me if I were not so wholly modelled on her, for she suffered from crippling rheumatic pains in her legs, and so did I. Sometimes in our house in Pócsi Utca we would be moaning almost in unison: 'Oh, my legs! My legs!'

My mother believed that she had developed rheumatic pains in her legs after travelling during winter in unheated trains. But I had not journeyed in an unheated train in the middle of the Hungarian winter, so where did my leg pains come from? The doctor who was called on occasions to examine me came up with the not unreasonable theory that, in resembling my mother in so many ways, I also resembled her in sources of suffering. The pain was very real. I remember long nights with my mother or my father rubbing my aching limbs with methylated spirits. I recall the smell of the spirits, but not any relief that came my way through its application.

Proper relief for the pain was found at Hajdúszoboszló, the town where we had family holidays. It was home to a resort called Szoboszló, famous for the therapeutic properties of its natural springs. Often it was just Mother and me who travelled to Hajdúszoboszló during the summer. We went by train, and as we neared the town the pleasant reek of the mineral waters reached me and my heart raced. The waters were warm, and we would lean back and float, growing less and less rheumatic as the minutes passed. The benefit of these mineral baths I accepted without question, and the pain abated when we bathed at Szoboszló. I suppose part of the thrill of bathing at Szoboszló was simply that I had my mother to myself.

Approximately three thousand Jews lived in Nyírbátor, or around a quarter of the town's population. Such a high percentage was unusual in Hungary. I grew up with Jews to my north, south, east and west, to my left and right, ahead of me and behind me. So my impression was that we were more numerous than we were, in fact. Jewish culture and Jewish traditions were constantly before my eyes. Until the late 1930s, my impression was that it was as natural to be Jewish as to be anything else. I did not feel marginalised, although I was increasingly conscious of a level of disdain.

Three synagogues – Liberal, Orthodox and Hassidic – served the community; the worshippers chose their membership according to their taste or their traditions. My family belonged to the Orthodox congregation, the largest of the three. All members of the Orthodox congregation were, as you would expect, strict Sabbath observers. Our stern rabbi came from the famous Teitelbaum dynasty of the Szatmár region. Every Jew in Nyírbátor listened to what he had to say, whether or not they belonged to the Orthodox congregation. He ordered the Jews of the Liberal synagogue to close their shops on the Sabbath – a rule amongst the Orthodox that Liberal Jews might have been happy to ignore – and they did as he told them. The Liberal synagogue, with its beautiful stained-glass windows, was a far more aesthetically pleasing piece of architecture than the dour Orthodox *shul*, but it wasn't as well-attended. The assimilated Jews of the Liberal synagogue took their religious obligations far less seriously than the God-fearing Orthodox Jews, and most only went to *shul* on the high holy days. The more prosperous and sophisticated Jews of Nyírbátor were better represented in the Liberal congregation than amongst the Orthodox.

The Orthodox *shul*, then, a little dowdy on the outside, was also fairly utilitarian on the inside. I attended it only occasionally as a child. I visited the Liberal *shul* at a fairly young age and preferred it. Those at the Orthodox synagogue, coming from the poorer families of the town, dressed with less flair, and their grooming in general was less impressive. At the age I was then, good grooming suggested superiority.

The Hassidic *shul* remained something of a mystery to me. It was even more unprepossessing than the Orthodox synagogue. My sisters and I knew the children of the Hassidim, since they attended the Jewish elementary school, but they kept pretty much to themselves, dressed in their black garb. They made me somewhat uneasy, as if they didn't understand the ordinary mechanisms of friendship, or didn't wish to understand them.

The poorer Jews of Nyírbátor let their children's education lapse after the six years of Jewish day school, but the children of middle-class families went on to the non-Jewish high school for a further four years of education. The girls' high school I attended after my tenth birthday was not Jewish. There was nothing special about the school, except for the quality of instruction, which was of a truly high standard. My mother wanted her daughters to enjoy all the education available to them, knowing as she did that four years of high school was as far as Marta and Erna and I could go, as a university career was closed to us.

At the high school I had seven teachers, each specialising in one subject – mathematics, history and so on. Other than the headmaster, all my teachers were female, quite young, and all took their profession seriously. The headmaster, a Catholic priest, taught us German. (His background was German, in fact, and he would within a few years reveal himself to be a rabid anti-Semite.) I adored my secondary school with the same vigour that I'd displayed in my primary school years. All around me at the high school were girls who also relished learning. We were ready each day to be enlightened. Amongst the students were a group we spoke of as 'incomers'. These were girls who caught the train into Nyírbátor from outlying villages, then walked to the school from the station, which was some distance. They were lovely, serious girls, diligent and ambitious, and I admired their commitment.

I was weaker in maths than in other subjects. I enjoyed the humanities more, and especially the art classes we had. I recall one of my pictures with special affection. The subject was given to us as Easter approached: the Easter bunny, with painted eggs scattered around, and two children, a boy and a girl, the intended recipients of the coloured eggs, smiling in anticipation. I was around twelve at this time. We were permitted to work on the picture away from school, and so one afternoon in early April, after returning from school, I was out in our garden with my paints and brushes. Everything about my picture pleased me: the shapes I had fashioned of bunny, boy, girl; the colours I'd chosen; the relation of the figures to each other. All around me, the greenery of our garden glittered in the sunlight. I experienced a deep sense of self-approval for what I'd rendered, a type of bliss very much like the creative joy I'd felt when composing poetry *ex tempore* at our kitchen table years earlier. I was barely conscious of anything but my picture, the smell of the paint, and the green blur that surrounded me. I heard my mother calling me as the afternoon light faded and dusk arrived: 'Baba! Come inside, it's cold!' She called once, twice, five times, and each time I applied myself to my task with greater dedication. Cold? What did 'cold' matter when I was thoroughly enjoying myself? But my mother's cries became more insistent, carrying that note of true annoyance that I dreaded. And so, with the greatest reluctance, I called it a day and went inside.

We Jewish girls attended school on Saturdays also, under the proviso that we should not be made to write, as it was forbidden. According to the strictures of Judaism, when we reached the age of twelve we were not to carry anything on the street on the Sabbath. This was a problem, but not insurmountable. One of our friends would come to our house and, as a favour, carry our bags to school, and then back again.

For us Orthodox girls, there were few chances to get together with boys, or even to speak to them. We didn't go to dance classes, for instance, where we might have come face-to-face with a boy. And there was no opportunity to glance at boys at the swimming pool – and receive glances in return – since we were unwelcome there. It would have been heaven to meet an attractive boy who not only took an interest in me as a girl – and I was quite pretty, if I may say so without sounding vain – but who also revealed a profound interest in the destination of the soul of the flea. Imagine – attraction and philosophy combined!

The eccentric Rabbi Lemberger provided religious instruction to the Jewish girls of the high school. He was an old man with a white beard. We attended his service in the Liberal synagogue on Saturday mornings – and we attended in droves. It wasn't that we hungered for enlightenment, but rather that the synagogue offered us a glimpse, from the women's gallery, of the boys below. Our hope was that they might glance up at us every now and again. Each of us girls had our favourite boy, and the boy whose glance inflamed my heart was Miki. He was fourteen, a year older than me.

For the whole of that time in Rabbi Lemberger's synagogue, my life was seeing Miki. Wooing, tender words of endearment – all were magically captured in those glances, and never a word spoken between us. When I lay in bed at night I did not think of Miki; I was too deeply occupied with sorting through questions of theology, and with attempting to solve existential conundrums. But the thrill of seeing his face for two seconds on Shabbat morning, his eyes seeking out mine … My memories of Miki are still sweet and clear today.

CHAPTER 7

Sources of Delight

If my mother had kept a diary, it would have been a thing of beauty. Her handwriting was exquisite. My mother took great pride in her employment of language, and held it pretty much a sin to show any negligence: she would never permit a single error in grammar or an ill-chosen word. The care she took reflected her reverence for what could be achieved with language – the art of the great writers.

I have already written fondly of my own love of literature. As in any love affair, one can recall certain peaks of intensity. Once, while visiting my maternal grandparents, I came upon a small bookshelf in a corner of the living room. On it I discovered a dozen large volumes, containing bound copies of a weekly magazine for girls, *Magyar Lányok* ('Hungarian Girls'). Each volume held a year's worth of issues. I had never seen the magazine before, and indeed it was no longer published; these issues had

Preparing to go to a wedding.
Back row from left: Baba, Marta, a maid, Klari (Lipe's wife and Boeske's
sister-in-law). Front row from left: unknown, cousin Mira Kellner.
Mira was holding Baba's hand during Mengele's selection, as we will read later.

From left: Mira again, baby Kati, Klari and Mimi Kellner.

been purchased for my mother and her sisters before the First World War.

I opened a volume and flicked through it: stories, poems, articles that told of the history of Hungary and other lands. The pages, although yellow with age and devoid of coloured illustrations, gleamed for me. Just one issue of *Magyar Lányok* would have thrilled me, but fifty-two issues in a single volume, and twelve volumes! This was a blessing fallen from heaven and I was crazy with excitement. I asked and was permitted to bring the volumes back to our own house.

Each time I opened a volume to read the issues, I breathed in that transporting tang of paper in its infinitely slow decay – a preface to the even greater pleasure of plundering the stories and articles. I did not have to wait weeks to read each instalment of a story that captivated me, as my mother would have waited; I could turn to the continuation in the next issue, and the next. I read each issue twice, at least. It made not the slightest difference to me that I knew the conclusion to a story. I read late into the night, illuminating the pages of *Magyar Lányok* with the beam of a torch under my doona. Such was the allure of reading that I can still recall, seventy years later, some of the sentences I read in *Magyar Lányok*.

The magazines in their binders were not my only source of reading, of course. My mother kept a substantial library and I was free to make my choice from the shelves. And Nyírbátor had a lending library, a good one, with many foreign works translated into Hungarian. It was a private business run by the wife of our family dentist. Mother and I called in at the library regularly, and became so familiar with it that we more or less thought of its shelves of books as an extension of our home.

The reviews in the newspapers and magazines to which my mother subscribed kept us fairly well informed about recently published books. We knew who had won the Nobel Prize for Literature each year. We did not always know much about the winners of the prize, but we assumed that the books of the Nobel laureates would be wonderful to read. The newspapers and magazines also made us aware of the films and stage shows running in Budapest. It was not likely that we could travel to the capital to attend the theatre – we were not that fancy, or that well heeled – but still it was good to be *au courant* culturally. Nyír-bátor had a cinema, and we paid for our tickets and sat in that velvety darkness every now and again. The movies were usually popular fare. I was no intellectual snob – I was as interested in gossip about actors and actresses as in Nobel laureates.

At the age of twelve, I myself was a keen young actress. It was a further outlet for the creative urge in me, and one I could not resist. On the stage, with so many pairs of eyes appreciating my prettiness, my craft, my ability to retain perfectly the lines of my character – I relished it. Indeed, no play in our high school could be performed without me, and I took to the stage with the demeanour of a diva, full of self-confidence. My greatest role was in a play in which I commanded two roles: a grandmother and a fairy.

The play called for me first to appear as the shrivelled grand-mother, stooped and hobbling, getting along with the aid of a walking stick. At a certain point in the unfolding drama, I was transformed into a radiant fairy.

The latter role called for a certain amount of nimble dancing, which was not one of my talents. My teacher, Miss Lenke, sent me along to private dance classes to help me prepare. The lessons had to be private, because Jewish kids were not welcome at the regular classes. My parents were not concerned about their daughter dancing alongside gentile kids at school, I'm happy to say, and I was permitted to attend the classes. But after my private instruction, Miss Lenke asked me to stay on and take part in her class for the other children of Nyírbátor – the children who were not Jewish. And I adored the experience. A circle was formed, boys and girls paired. This was the closest I had ever been to a boy, and even though my boy, on that day, was not the divine Miki, he did nicely enough. I attended four dance classes and relished every minute. But that was it. I had mastered my dance for the play, so there was no further reason – no further *excuse* – for me to go along.

When I was thirteen, my beloved Miss Lenke gave me a poem to recite on Mother's Day. I read through the text with mounting disappointment. It was a decidedly pedestrian piece of work – short, lifeless, a concatenation of platitudes. What opportunity would this forgettable stuff provide for me to shine on stage? So I decided to surprise Miss Lenke by reciting another poem

A family day trip in 1939 to the Hungarian territories, recently returned from Slovakia.
Standing, from left: Boeske, Janni Krammer (Gyula's first cousin),
his wife, Illus, and Erna.
Sitting, from left: Marta, Baba, Gyula and the driver (obscured by smoke).

altogether, one suitable for Mother's Day but much more engaging. I studied the text of my poem closely, and three days before the recital I went to Miss Lenke and told her, very tactfully, that the poem she had chosen left a great deal to be desired. I then recited my alternative poem, and Miss Lenke was thrilled. On the day of the recital, I stood on stage, gave a wonderful rendition of the poem and was able to enjoy the sight of my mother, seated in the audience, beaming with pride as I made my curtsies.

Not everything I involved myself in creatively brought the reward of applause. One of my more homely pursuits at that time was embroidery, a craft that my sisters and I practised assiduously. Hungary had long been home to beautiful embroidery. Patterns varied from region to region, or even within regions. We learned a number of different stitches and techniques, all traditional, under the tutelage of our schoolteacher and our mother, who had herself been perfecting her embroidery since childhood. Tablecloths, serviettes, blouses, dresses, handkerchiefs, scarves – we took on everything. In Hungary it was accepted that any piece of cloth, whatever its use, could surely be improved by being embroidered. I recall times of blessed peace when we all worked together with our embroidery on our laps or within a frame, a perfect feminine harmony of endeavour: my mother singing, and nothing in the world to distract us.

The craft of embroidery became the answer to a problem that my parents had to face once Erna had finished high school. Five years older than me, she was barred from attending university and so needed an occupation until she married, which might not be for a few years. My parents decided to open a shop in the town centre. My mother would be the proprietor. Erna was sent to Budapest for a year – this was in 1938 – to complete an advanced apprenticeship in the art of embroidery at a ladies' finishing school.

A building was leased when Erna returned from Budapest. It was fitted out with a long wooden counter, handsome timber shelves, tables and chairs. A large window faced the street, and in the window all manner of embroidered items were on display. A sign was hung: 'Erna's Handwork Shop'. The shop attracted customers, but running a business in a way that actually afforded a profit was not amongst my mother's talents. In her generosity, she extended credit to people who couldn't or wouldn't repay her, and at the end of each month my father was compelled to make up the difference between the shop's income and its outgoing expenses. The shop was one half a business, one half a social meeting place.

Our house in these years was often transformed into a type of salon, where Jews from the town, women and girls, for the most part, gathered to enjoy my mother's hospitality and conversation. I was there, soaking in the atmosphere, attending to what three or four voices were saying at the one time. We were all knitting, comparing patterns, laughing easily, perhaps listening to music, too. My mother was always at the heart of the gathering, not by intention but by virtue of her charisma. I could see why my father so adored her, even if the chatter of these gatherings drove him crazy. My father did not overflow with the joy of life, as my mother did; he was quieter, more reserved.

This life I am revealing – this father, this mother, this family – is the life I would wish for everyone. No harm in any of us, but instead a sense of the inexhaustible sources of delight in the world. Yes, if I could bestow a gift on others, it would be to live as my family had lived before the great darkness. Let everyone know what it was to bask in the love and care of such a mother and such a father. Let everyone know what it was to have Erna and Marta as sisters.

Baba, aged fifteen, in May 1943.

CHAPTER 8

A Speck of Light

Beyond my life with my family in Nyírbátor, of course, the approach of war in Europe was quickening. News reached us of the German onslaught and atrocities enacted against Jews, and we were well aware of the growing anti-Semitism in Hungary. My family, and all the Jews of Nyírbátor, felt increasingly menaced.

By late 1940 Europe belonged to Hitler. His armies occupied France, Belgium, Denmark, the Netherlands, Czechoslovakia and half of Poland. In Italy, Hitler's ally Mussolini was in power. In Spain, Franco, a great admirer of the man who bombed Guernica, supported Hitler without actually committing Spanish troops to fight alongside German troops. The leaders of Bulgaria, Romania and Hungary took their orders from Hitler, while Prince Paul of Yugoslavia was prepared to do whatever he must to appease the Axis powers.

We had seen the darkness grow. But we thought: 'It will not come here.' Even as we had such thoughts, we knew that we were deceiving ourselves. Jews were being deported from Hungary for lacking citizenship papers, and they departed in a wretched state. Other Jews arrived from the German occupied countries around us, from Poland or Slovakia, and told us of the horrors they'd seen. A cousin came to Nyírbátor from Bratislava with a story of young Jewish women there who had been taken to the front to satisfy the lust of the German soldiers. We hoped Hitler would be defeated. But perhaps there was more to the unwillingness of my family, and of so many other Jewish families, to flee the danger. A type of inertia ties people to the soil on which they have stood for so long.

When I was fourteen, a letter came from an address in the Slovakian territories (newly restored to Hungarian rule by the generous Germans). The sender's name was Mädy; she was my age and she wanted a pen-friend. To find a correspondent, she turned to her distant relative in my town, the spinster daughter of a Jewish teacher, who gave her my name. I was flattered, but also simply glad. A pen-friend – yes, I could enjoy that.

I wrote back to Mädy and told her about myself, my town, my family. She replied, offering the same sort of information. She lived in the town of Huszt, away to the north-east, bigger than Nyírbátor but by no means a thriving city. After a number of letters each way, we made plans to visit each other. Mädy came to Nyírbátor first, during the school holidays. Later, I visited her in Huszt, and stayed for two weeks. She had two sisters; one wore a metal frame of the sort employed at that time for children recovering from polio. Mädy was a jolly girl, full of fun, fond of jokes, but we didn't quite share the intellectual interest I had hoped we would. Mädy made a second visit to Nyírbátor the following year, but I declined a second visit to Huszt. It wasn't that my family thought it too dangerous for me to leave Nyírbátor, but our sense of siege may have contributed to my reluctance to go north again.

One of our neighbours was Mrs Graber, the mother of ten children. Mrs Graber had come to Nyírbátor from Poland. She could not provide proof of Hungarian citizenship and was deported by the state to Poland, leaving her ten children behind with Mr Graber. By some miracle Mrs Graber managed to return, and she had seen things in Poland that would haunt her forever: Jews in their thousands digging deep trenches with shovels and picks. The Germans would then make them kneel at the lip of the trench, and would shoot each person in the back of the head. This is what Mrs Graber witnessed.

Any war creates a graveyard of hopes and longings. My sister Erna, fair-haired and beautiful, met a young man by the name of Lajos, who came from Mátészalka. Lajos was tall and handsome, and he and Erna fell in love. Erna had been in Szoboszló running a small kiosk on behalf of my mother's half-sister, Anna, who had fallen ill with what turned out to be tuberculosis. One fine day, along came Lajos, and one way or another a warm friendship developed. His family owned a hat factory, so it might be expected that he could make a good living, and he was only two or three years older than Erna, so he was accepted as a suitor. My sister was happy, of course – more than happy.

When the time came for her handsome young man to visit our family at Nyírbátor, everything seemed ripe for an engagement. Ahead of his arrival, Lajos sent his sweetheart a huge basket of flowers, pink hydrangeas, rare in Hungary. Lajos included a note with his tribute: 'Flowers for a golden flower.' Marta and I were amused, but I also approved of the sentiment and thought it romantic. Lajos asked my father for permission to marry Erna. My father discussed the proposal with my mother for about thirty seconds, then informed Lajos that, indeed, he could take Erna as his wife.

The wedding day was set for June of that year, 1942. Our family visited Lajos's family, and then there was a reciprocal visit. The planning for the marriage went ahead, and also for Shavuot, the sixth day of the Hebrew month of Sivan, when Jews commemorate the revelation of the Torah to the assembled Jewish nation at Mount Sinai. Shavuot is mostly a day of feasting and smiles but Lajos had some awful news to share with Erna, news he kept to himself throughout the Shavuot rites. He had been called up for Labour Service.

Young Jewish men were no longer permitted to serve with the regular Hungarian armed forces; instead, they were required to join the Labour Service and dig trenches, latrines and the like.

In short, they had to devote themselves to the most menial tasks of all. Their rations barely kept them alive, and if they were injured or fell ill, they would receive next to no medical aid. On the battlefield, they became human minesweepers, sent out into fields known to be sown with landmines; many would be blown to pieces.

With his Labour Service unit, Lajos was sent to the Eastern Front in Russia. Erna, desolate in Nyírbátor, waited for a light-green postcard from him – cards issued at the front that allowed for no more than a few words of news. She treasured these rare gifts from her husband-to-be. What Lajos conveyed in his few permitted words was a few weeks old by the time she received them. The cards Lajos sent Erna were smudged with his tears.

(At the end of 1944, what was left of Lajos's Labour Service battalion was marched right through Hungary to Germany. We heard more than a year later that Lajos died on that death march; his body was thrown to the side of the road.)

I recall the summer of 1942 more vividly and in more detail that any season during the years of growing danger. I recall the warm winds that carried the fragrance of blossoms. I recall flirting with boys with intense delight on the long evenings. The dusk crept over us by such slow degrees that the darkness settled without our noticing it. We left the street reluctantly – left our games, left the boys avid for more of our teasing, our smiles. Each evening, as I entered our house, I hoped that tomorrow would be as enthralling as was today.

I was happy, and I loved life and its bounty. But at the same time, I was a thinking, growing person, facing all the tribulations typical of my fourteen years, and more. Questions flooded into my mind, and they seemed so urgent, almost as if life could not continue until I found the answers. Some were profound and existential, to do with the obligations of a human being in the world; others were religious, relating to faith and belief. I longed for a friend with whom I could talk about the troubles that beset me, but I had no friends who would find any natural sympathy with the things I wished to discuss.

I had a loving relationship with my mother, and we could talk happily about books, clothes and boys. But I did not dare raise the subject of religion. My mother brought me up to honour our beliefs in exactly the way prescribed by the fathers of our Orthodox faith. She considered the rites and rules of our faith to be fairly much beyond analysis or enquiry. There was a way to live, a way to worship, a way to be a Jew. I doubt she thought that any good could come from critical scrutiny or introspection.

It was not the same for me. I desperately wanted answers that would resolve my doubts. There was nothing wanton about this; I hadn't gone out looking for contradictions in the tenets of my faith merely to be contradictory. No, my doubts were simply the product of a reflective intelligence. Some were rooted in basic logic. If the Jews were chosen by God from amongst all the peoples of the earth, surely that meant that there was a hierarchy of races in heaven. This seemed to me to mar the concept of the family of man. I had other doubts, too, about the intentions and ambitions of God, and I could not shrug them off. My arguments with my faith led me into a wilderness of despair. But these were heavy thoughts that would get in the way of the enjoyment of my days, and I remember collecting them as they came to my mind and putting them off until the nights.

At the age of fourteen I finished my formal education. But I longed to continue my studies. It seemed my destiny to learn, and to thrive in my learning, but now I was thwarted. I knew that tears would not change my circumstances. There was no school for higher education in my town, and I had no prospect of attending a non-Jewish school in a nearby town. All the Jewish high schools were far away from us, and they did not offer dormitories for students from remote towns such as Nyírbátor.

So I just kept on reading: an unstructured education, but better than nothing. I was both student and teacher.

Baba, aged fifteen, in 1942. The photo was taken by Kati Lichtmann, then a student of photography. On the back of the photo is Kati's handwritten declaration: 'Isten nevében kezdem el' (In God's name I start my work). This photograph was not buried, but kept safe by a neighbour.

CHAPTER 9

Mishi's News

When from 1938 Jews who could not prove that they were Hungarian citizens began to be deported, my father searched for the documents that would save us from the same fate. He found documents showing that in 1820 the Hungarian authorities had issued a permit allowing one of our Keimovits ancestors to open an inn at 1 Pócsi Utca, Nyírbátor, Szabolcs-Szatmár-Bereg county, Kingdom of Hungary. Many other Jews were not so lucky. For the lack of a slip of paper, their lives were overtaken by wretchedness and poverty; many died at the hands of the anti-Semitic Hungarian 'Guardians of Order'.

In any such crisis as this, men and women take upon themselves the burden and danger of bringing relief. Periodically, many Jews, young and old, were rounded up at random and taken to various holding camps. My mother's sister Marta lived in Budapest. Armin, her husband, was forever occupied with looking after those who remained, who were liable, on any day, to be taken from their homes by the police or by gendarmes. Armin became a one-man relief agency, finding places to hide those in danger, feeding them with kosher food, offering words of encouragement. How Armin still managed to make a living, I can't imagine. It was said in our household that he was devoted to his heroic role all day, every day.

Lajos, Erna's sweetheart, was one of tens of thousands of Jewish men who were conscripted into the Labour Service in 1942. Sons and bridegrooms, fathers and breadwinners, all sent to Russia under the command of the Hungarian army. By early 1943, I doubt there remained a single Jewish family in Hungary that was not mourning the death, deportation or conscription of a relative or a close friend at the hands of the Hungarian army. The darkness had deepened. And Hungarian Jews were better off than Jews in other European countries. It was said that the Hungarian Regent, Horthy Miklós, accepted very large bribes from wealthy Jews not to order the rounding up of all Hungarian Jews. But the distinction between the lucky and the unlucky Jews of Hungary was steadily shrinking. My father and mother did not want to imagine the time, now not far ahead, when all the Jews of Hungary would be wretched, starving, condemned to death.

By mid-March of 1944, I was more a young woman than a child. I had celebrated my sixteenth birthday three months earlier. Yet my understanding of the situation we were in had not changed radically. For six years now I'd been conscious that the danger we faced was increasing. The incremental adjustments I had made meant I was as prepared as I could be for whatever was coming next. Only let the next change be nothing too severe, I prayed. Let me continue to enjoy Sundays with my friends, and with my mother's friends, who gathered at our house for games and conversation, girls as well as boys. Above all, let my cousin Mishi be amongst us: so good-looking, so well built, a carefree boy with an infectious laugh and a wealth of jokes to share.

Sunday the nineteenth of March, however, was unlike any other Sunday I had experienced. And I was not able to assimilate the news that Mishi brought with him. He knocked on our door much earlier than we were prepared for; my mother said, with a puzzled expression, 'At this hour? Who would arrive as early as this?' She hurried to the door, with me close behind.

Mishi stood on the verandah, a horrified expression on his face. 'Auntie Boeske, the Germans!'

My mother tried to calm him down. 'Mishi, come inside. Please, make some sense. What about the Germans?'

'The Germans are taking over Hungary! Even now they are taking over Hungary.'

'Where did you hear this, Mishi?'

'In the town. Everybody knows. They are marching into Budapest. Many, many soldiers on foot with guns. Even now.'

It was not so much Mishi's news that shocked me as Mishi himself. This was not the boy whom we all knew. No jokes now, no banter, no smiles. I was used to the daily bombast of the

Hungarian troops marching through Nyírbátor, singing their hateful songs at the tops of their voices. Those words now become a message of intent, and the full horror of that message was visible on Mishi's face. *'Hey, Jew, hey, Jew, hey, you stinking Jew, What are you doing here amongst us Hungarians?'* The question now seemed to provide its own answer.

The expression on Mishi's face that morning brought back to me an incident from a year earlier, when I was travelling by train to visit a friend. I had struck up a conversation with a young Hungarian man seated opposite me. This fellow, not yet in uniform, told me that he had been called up for military service in the Hungarian army.

'And where will you be sent to?' I asked him. He was a pleasant young fellow.

'Where will I serve? In a place called Nyírbátor. I have to report to Nyírbátor barracks shortly. I don't know anything about the place.'

'Oh, that's where I live!' I said, surprised and delighted by the coincidence. 'That's my home town.'

'Really? Then you can tell me about it. What's it like?'

'Pretty measly,' I said, meaning simply that Nyírbátor was fairly small and insignificant.

The ticket conductor was standing nearby and overheard my answer. It threw him into a rage. 'Stinking Jewess!' he shouted for all to hear. 'How dare you call a Hungarian town measly! Our motherland! How dare you!' He wanted to throw me off the train.

Some passengers who witnessed this rabid outpouring took my side, and told the conductor he would do no such thing. Others were fully in favour of punishing me with eviction for the gross crime of referring to Nyírbátor as 'measly'. In the end, I was permitted to remain on the train, but it was a close-run thing. The idea that any hyper-patriot could give vent to this sort of anti-Semitic rant without being thought mentally unstable stayed with me.

Not much later than that episode, I was making another train journey, perhaps even along the same route. I stood in a carriage full of passengers while a group barely a metre away discussed my possible origins in an animated way. *'Is she a Jew? Of course she's a Jew! I'm not so sure. Dear God, can there be any doubt – she's a Jew!'* I gazed out of a window, pretending I heard nothing, but my sense of injustice was inflamed. What I could not say, but wished with all my being that I could, was this: 'A Jew – yes, I am a Jew, and I thank God that being a Jew distinguishes me from people such as you!'

The danger I was in when the conductor abused me came back when Mishi stood pale and trembling in our hallway, telling us his dreadful news. I already knew how serious our situation was, but the disdain and violence in the conductor's face merged in my mind with an image of soldiers marching into Budapest, and I knew something horrible lay ahead.

I must have had a sort of premonition three months earlier, on the eve of my sixteenth birthday. That night, I'd been unable to fall asleep. I lay in the warmth and comfort of my bed, sobbing my heart out. On the night of the fourteenth of December, 1943, the slow build-up of danger I'd been experiencing overwhelmed me. I was mourning the end of my childhood, saying goodbye to the first part of my life and anticipating the perilous future.

The Germans changed the Hungarian government on the day they marched into Budapest. The puppet government immediately enacted anti-Jewish laws and sanctions even more severe than those already in place. The Germans, after establishing what was expected, preferred to leave the persecution of the Jewish population to the Hungarians. And what was expected was what had been done in other European countries the Nazis had occupied or dominated. The catalogue of abuses taking place in Austria, Germany, Romania, France, the Netherlands, Slovakia and Belgium – arrests, detention, outright murder – was now to be visited upon Hungarian Jews.

An especially brutal arm of the Hungarian national police – the gendarmes, as they were called – was given responsibility for rounding up Jews. The gendarmes were greatly feared in Hungary, and not only by Jews: they were capable of behaving vilely towards anyone. But they took a special relish in persecuting Jews, and were urged on in this by their Nazi masters.

Bad news came thick and fast. Day after day, we heard about new regulations, new restrictions, new demands. The Hungarians were obsessed with their 'Jewish question', and worked on nothing else but the Jewish laws. The German troops in Budapest made it more urgent that the Hungarians should find ways to show their compliance, but the smug looks on the faces of the gendarmes in their rooster-plumed helmets advertised their delight in enforcing the new laws. They had been waiting for this.

The authorities demanded that in all towns and villages a *Judenrat*, or 'Jewish Council', be established. Eight or nine leaders of the Jewish community were to be selected in each town, or in each congregation in the cities. These people would be the contact between the administrators and the Jewish population. My grandfather, Ignac Kellner, seventy-three years old, was a member of the nine-man *Judenrat* of Nyírbátor.

One law passed after the arrival of the Germans made it mandatory for all Jewish families to surrender their jewellery, and also any radios they owned, to the authorities. In Nyírbátor the Town Hall was to be the depository of these possessions. We knew this was simply legalised theft. We would never see the jewellery again, never have our radios returned. How I sorrowed for the loss of our radio! Where would our news come from now? We would hear nothing but that which the authorities wanted us to hear: propaganda and lies.

From the fifth of April, every Jew was ordered to wear a yellow star, which had to be sewn to whatever outer garment he or she wore, on the left side, above the heart. It was emphasised that the yellow star must be clearly visible. Our household was full of females expert in the use of needle and thread, but I can't remember the actual sewing on of the yellow stars. I am sure we did sew the stars on; to have defied the authorities would have been court-ing disaster. That was something we now understood: we could be killed by the Hungarians, probably the gendarmes, and there would be no enquiry, no coroner's report. We would live or die according to the wishes of people who hated us.

Pesach came, the festival of Jewish freedom: the Children of Israel, the Exodus from Egypt three thousand years ago, deliv-erance from slavery, the birth of a nation. It was obligatory for the heirs of those wanderers who made that journey with Moses to remember, and to retell, the days of slavery and redemption.

With all the agonising worries, our mother prepared a kosher Pesach Seder. We chanted the traditional verses of the Haggadah. And, following tradition, at the beginning of the night the young-est participant – Marta – started singing 'The Four Questions':

Ma nishtanah halailah hazeh mikol haleilot?
Sheb'khol haleilot anu okhlin hametz umatzah; halailah
hazeh, kuloh matza ...

Why is this night different from all other nights?
On all other nights we eat both chametz and matzah; on this
night, we eat only matzah ...

On the night of our last Seder before the catastrophe, there was another difference: my father was unable to read, let alone chant the text. He wept right through the ceremony. He knew clearly what the future could hold; he had been a prisoner of war for two years during the First World War. He knew, but he was powerless to protect his family, and that overwhelmed him. I saw his tears run down his cheeks at that Seder, and my heart within me ached.

Ignac Kellner, Boeske's father and Baba's grandfather.

CHAPTER 10

The Road to Simapuszta

It was on that Pesach night that Nyírbátor's authorities chose to test the town's newly installed air-raid sirens. Everyone had been instructed what we should do when the siren sounded but when we heard that wailing at our Seder table, we remained where we were for a short time. It was as if we needed an extra minute before we could accept the shame of leaving our Seder. I looked at my father's face, at his ashen cheeks. Mingled with my love for him was a profound pity. As if he had not already suffered enough indignity.

We filed out into the chill of the spring evening and stood huddled together, my father still sobbing, and my mother too. We were mournful. When we returned to our Seder, we were in a mood that made us especially sympathetic to the Jews of Egypt when they heard Moses and Aaron commanding them to quit their homes and put their feet to the road of flight. But we did not have a Moses, and we had no place to go.

The next day, the nine members of Nyírbátor's *Judenrat*, including my grandfather, were informed that the entire Jewish population was to be transported to ghettoes in other towns. Not one Jewish soul would be permitted to remain. And the nine men of the *Judenrat* were ordered to keep this news to themselves. If they shared what they had been told with other Jews, they were told, they would be punished severely. Well, the nine men immediately shared their knowledge with their families, and within a short time every Jew in Nyírbátor understood what awaited them. How could these men have kept such news to themselves? They had been placed in an impossible position, and they chose the punishment they had been warned about. They must have thought it was preferable to betraying their fellow Jews.

Knowing now that they were to be taken a long way from their homes, the Jews of Nyírbátor began a frantic concealment of whatever valuables they had that were capable of being hidden: any remaining jewellery, gold, silver, family heirlooms – items too precious for the feeling invested in them to be abandoned to the thieves who would descend on their homes ten minutes after the owners' departure. Holes were dug in back gardens, in vacant fields; the hollows of trees were claimed as improvised vaults. The less pessimistic hid their valuables in the homes they would be abandoning – up in the ceiling, in nooks and crannies, in chimneys – hoping that they would one day return.

By this time we weren't living at 1 Pócsi Utca any more; we were renting elsewhere. Our landlady and her hunchback daughter gave us permission to bury a timber crate with our possessions in the backyard. My mother and father knew that our landlady and her daughter could be trusted: they liked and respected us. In the crate my mother stowed Erna's trousseau, silver cutlery, silver candelabras, jewellery, and the Meisen dinnerware that she so treasured; also clothing, furs, photographs, many odds and ends. And goose fat. My mother used goose fat in cooking and baking; she regarded it as indispensable. So she sealed some in a big enamel container and added it to the crate. A deep hole was required, and one was dug under cover of darkness. The crate was lowered in, and earth packed on top. The hole was a grave, and what was being buried was the life we had lived in Nyírbátor up until April 1944.

A great deal of digging and excavating was going on in Nyírbátor, and all this activity could not be hidden from the authorities. There would have been many reports to the gendarmes by non-Jewish neighbours. The gendarmes took the nine members of the *Judenrat* into custody, questioned them and beat them with fists and clubs and rifle butts – the punishment that had been promised. The savage beatings of the Jewish elders made wrecks of them. My grandfather Ignac was incapable of walking when he was finally allowed home. And old bones do not repair quickly. It is a terrible sorrow for me to recall, even to this day, that my grandfather's last weeks of life were riven with pain. He was a man whose dignity had shone out of his face all of his life. Very little dignity remains when one has been beaten like an animal.

The *Judenrat* informed us that we could take only what we could carry. We prepared for our next life – one in a ghetto – by making a rucksack for each member of our family. A whole houseful of furniture, pictures, books, utensils, ornaments, rugs, crockery, pots and pans, clothing, all reduced to what would fit in our rucksacks. Dishes from which we had eaten a thousand meals, rugs we had settled on with a book in hand – so many things in which we had invested our feelings. It wounded me to leave these things behind. And my mother was wounded even more deeply. For half of her life she had been a housewife, and she had built up this home for us, her children and her husband, by adding one more useful or beautiful thing. But she didn't weep as she sewed our sacks. She understood perfectly, I think, that we would all have to rely on her strength in the time ahead.

We packed food into our rucksacks too. We did not imagine that these people who were prepared to take our homes and belongings from us would undertake to feed us. Mother prepared special, nourishing foods for us to pack.

We made bigger bags for our bedding and pillows. Our busy hands distracted us just enough to keep despair at bay. 'Sew! Cut! Firmer stitches!' I told myself, and my mind made my hands obey. Thoughts of my poor, broken grandfather caused tears to well in my eyes. 'Sew! Cut! Firmer stitches!' I said again, and the thoughts were subdued.

By the morning of the twenty-first of April, we were ready. The rucksacks were packed. The gendarmes knocked loudly on our door at precisely nine o'clock, as they had said they would. They were not rough and cruel on this occasion; they were polite. 'Mr Keimovits, you and your family members are to report to the synagogue before being moved to another place for an indefinite period. This is by order of the military commander of the region. As you know, only such items as can be carried are permitted on the journey.' We walked out of our home, rucksacks on our backs and other bags in our arms.

My family was the first of all the Jewish families of Nyírbátor to be ordered to the synagogue. We were told by the gendarmes of their intention to take the wealthiest and most influential families first. They didn't say why, but I could guess. The authorities wanted to gratify the non-Jewish populace with some 'how-the-mighty-have-fallen' scenes. But my father was neither wealthy nor influential. These gendarmes, in choosing my family, were harking back to their peasant heritage: the fathers and grandfathers of those who became gendarmes were the sons of landless peasants who laboured all their lives in a hand-to-mouth existence. They were conditioned to believe that a man who owned cattle was, by definition, wealthy, and since my father dealt in the sale of cattle, he must therefore be the wealthiest Jew in Nyírbátor. So the gendarmes chose the Keimovits family to be removed first. (It took me some time to understand this; I was mystified for years.)

We walked to the synagogue under our burdens, armed gendarmes at either side. It was spring: the trees were coming into leaf, and the birds returning from their winter sanctuaries. How many times had I walked to school in this season of life renewed, carrying my school books, pausing every few steps to rejoice in the emerging greenery? Now I was bewildered. It was almost impossible for me to accept that our home was gone, and that the Hungarian Nazis had forced us onto this dreaded route. My fingers curled into a fist and one thought occupied my mind: 'I will return and I will have my revenge.'

Opposite the synagogue lived my grandfather Ignac. When we arrived at the synagogue, he, my Uncle Lipe, his wife Klara and their three daughters were standing at their gate. My grandfather was being supported by my uncle. They waved to us, the first family to be brought in. I raised my hand to wave back to my grandfather, uncle, aunt and cousins; it felt like an appeal.

Two of Nyírbátor's *shuls* – the Orthodox and the Liberal – were built side-by-side. The gendarmes directed us into the Liberal *shul*. Women of the town, non-Jews of course, had been ordered to wait at the entrance and search the belongings of all those who arrived. We placed our bags on the ground and waited wretchedly while these women went through them with busy fingers, giving cries of triumph when they found something that should have been forfeited to the authorities earlier. They threw whatever they confiscated into a corner – booty that would be divided amongst them at their leisure. More intimate searches would be conducted later, it was said. Midwives were on duty to probe the bodies of the women and girls. My mother, my sisters and I somehow escaped this ignominy.

More Jewish families arrived, then many more still, until the Liberal *shul* was full. On the faces of the adults I saw humiliation, despair, resignation, and here and there anger. The children, especially the smaller ones, were frightened and clung to their parents, sometimes also clutching a comforting toy. The older children, although just as terrified as their younger brothers and sisters, tried to look brave. Some even displayed a certain amount of resentment. The adults talked to each other, but not in the animated way that they would have if this had been a gathering before worship – of business, of interesting news from afar. No, this was conversation of a different sort.

I recognised many of the arrivals as the wealthier Jews of the town – businessmen and professionals. There was not one amongst them who looked as if he could take command, tell us to stiffen our spines, thrust out our chins. The mood of demoralisation was so pervasive that even small smiles of recognition when one family met another seemed out of place. I heard people murmur: 'What is to become of us?' Once the Liberal *shul* was full, the Orthodox *shul* was opened, and soon the flow of Jewish families filled it too. I had never seen so many of my faith gathered together in this way.

We knew that we wouldn't be kept for the rest of our days locked up in the two synagogues. At four o'clock the next morning, a long line of horses and carts pulled up outside. It appeared that every farmer in the region with a wagon to his name and a beast to draw it had turned up to earn whatever fee the town's administrators were paying. We were herded from the *shul* to the first of the carts, and told to hand our bags and backpacks up to the driver. Then we climbed aboard and sat on top of our baggage.

As the cart began the journey to wherever we were going, I saw the curtains of the houses that lined the way twitching: those inside were watching, no doubt enjoying our humiliation. The injustice of it burned in my chest. I whispered to myself again: 'I will return and have my revenge.' Those who were spying at us from behind their curtains seemed the most despicable of all.

The cart lurched along, forcing us to sway to keep our balance. The peasant driving the cart said nothing, and was apparently indifferent to whatever was going on with the Jews of Nyírbátor. He was being paid – perhaps that was all he thought about.

My father asked the driver: 'Where are you taking us? Where are we going?'

The driver said: 'Simapuszta.'

'Simapuszta?' my father asked. 'Why there?'

'The Jews are going to Simapuszta. That's all I know. The Jews are going to Simapuszta.'

We looked at each other, puzzled. Simapuszta? It was nothing – rural land, further north in the direction of Nyíregyháza. Why take us from Nyírbátor to Simapuszta? What was in Simapuszta?

The countryside we passed through was the common vista of the north-eastern plains. Meadows, crops, farmhouses that had stood for one or two or three centuries, cattle, pigs in muddy enclosures. The journey took maybe three hours, and when we arrived we found a broad, barren area enclosed by wire. Within the enclosed area stood a number of huge barns, and it was here we were expected to bed down. Tents had also been erected on the bare earth outside. The gendarmes bustled us into one of the barns, and a small patch of ground was designated as the area that would be occupied by the Keimovits family.

My mother didn't grumble or complain. She set to work laying our bedding, issuing instructions to Erna and Marta and me. On each side of our patch of earth, other families were doing the same thing. It was now late in the afternoon – almost evening – and my mother wanted to feed us from the provisions we had packed.

There were few gendarmes about; it was almost as if we were guarding ourselves. And where might we have run off to? Into the empty plains? No, if we'd thought of fleeing, we would have done it earlier – months or years earlier. There would be no running away now.

CHAPTER 11

Train

When I reflect on the weeks at Simapuszta, I see a strange, almost grotesque mixture of realities. We gossiped, we bantered, we made plans for the future, and we flirted. Well, I flirted, along with many other girls of my age. We didn't know, of course, that we were on the way to hell. But we might have deduced that the Germans intended to kill us all. If we had deduced that, would we have sat with our heads bowed and our cheeks wet? I don't know. We may still have chattered away, simply because we would not have believed that we were marked for death.

Ignac, Uncle Lipe, his wife and my cousins arrived at the camp two days later. They were assigned to an area a long way from us; the ghetto was vast. News of their arrival came to us from our neighbours, who'd picked it up from someone further away. We went to visit them as soon as we heard, as we were desperately worried about Grandfather's condition. He was bedridden, unable to move.

I had adopted a way of looking at our situation that made it possible for me to avoid despair: I took only short views and long views; nothing in between. The short view showed me still alive; my mother and father, Marta and Erna were all still healthy and breathing. The long view projected me months or even years ahead, living in Nyírbátor again, the war over, the Nazis annihilated. I could shut out the time in between. But seeing my grandfather Ignac, broken and wracked with pain, reminded me that brutality was the first recourse of the gendarmes, and of their Nazi masters. If it suited their strategy to beat everyone in the camp in the way they'd beaten my grandfather, they would, without hesitation.

The gendarmes fed us nothing but a watery soup made by boiling potato peelings. It would have been possible to die of malnutrition even if you'd consumed gallons of that stuff each day. Most people had brought food with them, and those who hadn't were fed by those who had. Did we need any further proof that the Hungarians were unconcerned if we died? At meal times, my mother made us our own soup, more substantial than the camp soup. She had given thought to what would keep us alive not just for days, but for weeks.

'Girls, find a branch somewhere and sweep the ground,' she said. 'Pick up all the twigs from the sweepings and bring them to me.'

We did as we were told, and Mother used the twigs to start a small fire out in the open. She added larger pieces of wood to the blaze – where she came by them I cannot say – and heated the soup in a pot she'd brought from home. When the soup was ready, she called to all of us: 'Come and eat!' People as versatile as my mother can appear at their best in almost any situation. At home, she ruled the house with serene confidence; here in the camp, she adapted in whatever ways were required. Her competence never deserted her.

We also received food from a man my father knew, not a Jew, who came to the camp with bread and other foods. He was not paid to do this; it was act of friendship, of sympathy. And our relatives in Budapest, not yet detained, managed to send us a parcel of food by post! Amazingly, letters and parcels were still delivered to us.

So the camp of Jews from Nyírbátor and the region around became, over that first week of detention, a community of the oppressed. Family by family, a struggle was played out each day. Fathers and mothers strove to hold on to their remaining authority as parents. It was they who had to say, 'We will endure.' Not perhaps in those exact words, but with that message.

As in any community, rivalry and spite still held sway here and there. A few of our distant relatives were at the Simapuszta ghetto, quite poor families whom we rarely saw. Their poverty embittered them towards my father and his family. They rejoiced in the levelling that forced the 'rich' Keimovits family to struggle along with everyone else. They saw me sweeping for twigs, and they saw Mother with her sleeves rolled up, struggling to heat her soup, and they called out exultantly, 'Not so high and mighty now, are we? The hoity-toity family of Gyula Keimovits!' I didn't understand what they were talking about; it had to be explained to me. I was amazed.

Four weeks we spent in the Simapuszta ghetto, sleeping on the ground, sweeping the earth with twigs. It takes longer than four weeks for a life to become 'normal'. For me, 'normal' was still Nyírbátor: three meals a day, the comfort of a bedroom, of a mattress underneath me when I slept. It was Shabbat with all of its beloved rituals. It was my mother busy in the kitchen, my mother singing. The truth, if I had only known it, was that 'normal' no longer existed for me. A year of sweeping with twigs in the Simapuszta ghetto would never be normal.

Rumours ran through the camp about what was to happen to us. We were now well into the month of May, close to summer, a golden time in each year's calendar for me. I hoped that the war would end before the summer was over, so I could enjoy the warmth of the season back at home. But the rumours we were hearing spoke of a long journey by train to the north.

On the twenty-second of May, everyone in the camp was ordered to pack up their belongings, except for their bedding, and march to the railway station in Nyíregyháza, a distance of about fifteen kilometres. 'Why is the bedding to be left behind?' I wondered. 'Are we going to a place where beds and bedding are provided? Or are we going to a place where we will not be permitted to sleep?' We did as we were told. There were a thousand or more of us – we vastly outnumbered those who were issuing the orders – but we did not disobey. To rebel would have been futile: we would have been shot. And despite the rumours, we still had some hope that all would be well. Hope is tenacious.

From the Simapuszta ghetto we walked to the railway station in Nyíregyháza, carrying our rucksacks. My family kept close together and spoke little. Indeed, amongst the great throng marching to Nyíregyháza there was very little conversation. We were not baffled by the enmity of the Germans, nor by the eager complicity of the Hungarians. We were Jews, and this is what Jews suffered. Some survived, some perished.

A train with many carriages was waiting for us, not at the station itself but before the station, in a field. It was a train designed to carry cattle and the like. The carriages were made of horizontal planks of timber, once painted but now ancient and flaking. When the sliding door of each carriage was drawn open, the interior appalled us. There were no seats, and the carriages stunk to high heaven.

We looked at each other, all of us in the crowd beside the train, and on each face one could see a recognition that our lives meant nothing to those who had brought us here. The beasts that had once been conveyed in these carriages would have been going to slaughterhouses. And these carriages were now thought suitable for human beings. 'Seventy to a carriage,' the guards shouted. 'Seventy to a carriage!' Families were permitted to stay together. Fathers climbed into the carriages and reached down for their children, who were lifted up by their mothers. By this time there was fear in the air; many children were crying.

I clambered into a carriage with my backpack, then stood up and looked about quickly for Marta and Erna, who had gone ahead of me. My mother was already in the carriage too, and now Father climbed up and we were all together.

More and more people climbed into the carriage, and we were forced further and further back. 'Dear God, there is no more room,' I thought to myself. But there was more room: our carriage did not yet hold seventy people. We were pushed further in, away from the door, keeping track of each other out of the corners of our eyes. 'They can't treat people this way!' I thought. Despite all we'd been through, I hadn't fully accepted that the guards and the gendarmes could do anything they wished to do; that they were unrestrained by any humane consideration.

On the faces around me, I saw terror, resignation, exhaustion. I looked down at the upturned faces of children who only came up to my waist. They were hoping, I'm sure, for some guidance from the adults around them. If anything in the world can be considered to be simply wrong – for all people, at all times, regardless of culture or religion – it is to subject children to the sort of dread and confusion that the Jewish children in that train carriage experienced. That can never be other than wrong. We can't have a world unless we believe that.

The twenty or so carriages of the train were loaded with the Jews of Nyírbátor over a period of perhaps an hour. We all had to stand as there was not enough room for us to sit. We waited for whatever was to come next. The train began to move, very slowly at first, building up speed. I had travelled on trains many times before, of course. I had always enjoyed the moment when the train pulled out of the station, and I loved watching the scenery change. But this time my heart sank when I felt the train begin to move. 'People are not forced to travel in this way if the destination is anywhere good,' I thought. 'We are going to a bad place, I know it.'

Many aboard the train were weakened by hunger, having spent a month at the Simapuszta camp, and a number were ill. Those who were hungry became hungrier still. We ate what we had in our backpacks, and shared what we could with those who had nothing. It might be thought that a type of solidarity would develop in such a situation as ours, but in reality it did not. Sympathy, yes, but not true solidarity. My mother's great priority was to keep her children and her husband alive, so she fed us as best she could. It was the same for other mothers and families. There was no need to apologise for favouring one's own family; everyone understood, I'm sure.

For the sick and weak, a journey of three hours on their feet would have been an ordeal. This journey would last three days. All were exhausted by the ordeal, driven almost mad by the continual dread we felt, and by the endless clatter of the metal wheels.

People must relieve themselves, whatever the situation. Our toilets were buckets. On the first day of that nightmare journey, we managed some modesty when we were forced to use the buckets. As we squatted, a family member would shield us from view with a coat. But crammed together in a cattle car as we were, we soon came to see that modesty would have to be dispensed with. Some took longer than others to accept this necessity, but by the second day, coats were no longer held up to screen those using the buckets. Initially I felt shame, but I soon came to accept that it was our common lot – that I was one amongst seventy, and all of us were compelled to overcome our embarrassment.

Then the train came to a halt. In the course of the journey, I had registered other stops. Even in the near delirium of my exhaustion, I had known at times that we were not moving. Maybe the train drivers were changing over; maybe something was blocking the way. But the train always resumed its journey, slowly at first, then gathering speed until the *clack-clack-clack* of the wheels had returned to its regular, rapid interval. This time it was different.

I heard the release of steam from the engine, then silence. The tiny ventilation opening high on one of the walls of the carriage showed that it was dark outside. I'd been keeping track of time in a ragged way, and estimated that it was around four in the morning. It was the middle of spring and the days were lengthening.

'We've stopped,' I whispered to my mother. 'We have arrived.'

My mother didn't reply. I think all of us in the darkness of the carriage had sensed what I had, and shared the same feelings of anticipation and dread. Then I heard something like the clanking of a chain, very brief. After that, the silence grew more intense. I wanted to whisper to my mother again but I restrained myself.

What I did not know, what I could not have known, was that we had come to the gates of hell.

CHAPTER 12

Auschwitz

A dog barked, and this set off more barking, deep and booming, like that of hunting dogs. The barking alone frightened me, but soon we heard harsh voices as well, male German voices. Then came the rasp of metal on metal. The latch of the sliding door of our carriage was being unfastened. With great force, the door was hauled open.

We were not the closest to the doorway and at first I couldn't see the soldiers or the dogs, but people were spilling out of the carriage so quickly that it seemed only a very short time before I stood at the doorway with a flashlight beam in my eyes. I slid out of the carriage to the hard ground, already looking around in panic for my mother, my father, Erna and Marta. For a few moments I couldn't see them, then I could and a great rush of relief surged through me. I thought: 'Let me not be alone here, not alone, please God!' I reached out and seized hold of my father's arm, and held tight. Marta and Erna were with my mother, keeping very close.

All around was chaos. The dogs strained at their leashes, barking incessantly; the soldiers – the first German soldiers I had ever seen – pushed and shoved and shouted orders. The force they used was excessive. In the half-light of dawn, I could see that the other carriages were emptying too; the crowds on the ground beside each carriage were merging together. Amongst the German soldiers, certain officers seemed to have the greater authority. With shouted commands and with gestures, they made it understood that we were to separate into groups of male and female. Our belongings were to be dropped in a heap at a certain place. Twins – *Zwillinge* – were to form a special line. My father was forced away from the rest of us.

As we shuffled along, we were taken through some tall iron gates. Grim, three-storey brick buildings flanked the gates, and a barbed-wire fence, maybe six or seven metres high, enclosed the entire camp. We did not know the name of the place; indeed, we did not know what country we were in, except that it wasn't Hungary, not after three days of travelling north.

In the midst of our induction into Auschwitz on the twenty-sixth of May, while waiting for the next command, we were told in an urgent whisper by someone who had heard it from someone else that my mother's father, Grandfather Ignac, had been lifted from his carriage on the train and set down on the ground. He was asking for water; he was dying. It was impossible for us to get to him. I couldn't grieve then, but when it came, that postponed grief, it came with a terrible force.

We were searching amongst all of these frightened faces for my mother's sister-in-law, Klara, and her three daughters: Mira, who was twelve, Mimi, seven, and Kati, just three. Their nanny, Frieda, was also with them. We found them and I held Mira tight by the hand.

A tall, handsome German officer standing opposite the newly arrived Jews gestured with a wave of his hand which of two lines each of us was to join. What it meant if you were assigned to this line or that, we didn't know. The officer wore a blue-grey uniform, a long great-coat with epaulettes, and a peaked cap with a badge at the front. He seemed to me almost tranquil, perfectly satisfied in his task, with not a trace of malice. This man was Josef Mengele; one of his lines led to the dormitories, the other to the gas chambers.

A certain logic governed Mengele's decisions. Mothers with small children were directed to join one line; mothers with grown daughters – such as the four of us – were directed to the other. Small children could not labour in the way that would be required, and if mothers were forcibly separated from their small children, they would become wild with grief, and of no use. So it was better that the mothers went to their deaths with their children, so Mengele's logic said. Likewise, he sent the infirm and the aged to immediate deaths. Marta, Erna, Mother and I were all saved by this logic.

Mira was sent to our line; I was still holding her hand in mine. She wasn't looking at me but at all those in the other, bigger group. She was looking for her mother and sisters and nanny. She saw them in that crowd of the doomed. She released my hand and ran to join her family. I never saw her again. She would have gone up in smoke half an hour later.

I kept close to my mother and sisters, and also to Annushka, the pampered daughter of the well-off Mr Zeger, who ran the Bohny factory in Nyírbátor. We had been ordered by the SS officers to form ourselves into rows of five, and now that Mira was gone we needed another person to complete our group. My mother called to Annushka, who had been separated from her mother. 'Annushka! Come here! Come quickly!' The expression on Annushka's face showed her confusion and distress.

The SS officers made their will known by shouting commands and making emphatic gestures. They seized people and demonstrated with them what we were to do. What they now indicated was that we were to walk in a certain direction, keeping in our lines of five. We were urged along to a huge, wooden hall; inside, inmates with scissors were waiting for us. My instinct was to stop and gaze around, unwilling to go further until I understood what was happening. But I could not. The women waiting with scissors, row upon row of them, wore uniformly blank expressions. On the wooden floor at their feet were piles of human hair; it was evident what was about to be done to us.

Each of the inmates stood by a chair. We new arrivals were

bustled along to take a seat, and with no delay at all our hair was shorn from our heads. The woman who sheared me barely spoke. She lifted my soft, long locks and severed them quickly, moving my head to the left and right, forcing my head forward when she was working at the nape of my neck. I saw my hair falling to the floor, but I didn't mourn it. I was quite sure that I would be forced to endure worse experiences than this. I sat still, listening to the rapid clipping of hundreds of scissors, and to the shouted orders of the guards. 'Get a move on! Faster!'

Once shorn of our hair, we were ordered to undress. Hundreds of women and girls began to remove their clothing, in clear sight of the male SS guards. Sick with embarrassment, I tried to keep my gaze on the floor as I let my garments fall to my feet. I had lost sight of my mother and my sisters and was in a fever of anxiety. Inmates approached us with tanks of disinfectant and sprayed us where we stood, all over our bodies. In places where the scissors had caused wounds in the flesh of my scalp, the disinfectant stung badly. I heard other women and girls yelping as they too endured that stinging. And always the shouting of the guards.

Our induction was not yet finished. Big bundles of clothing were dumped on the floor, and inmates distributed garments to us. (I later realised that these garments had been owned by earlier arrivals, who by now were likely dead.) No attempt was made to match our height with the size of the garments. I was given a dress of jersey material patterned with colourful stripes, ludicrous to look at and far too big for me; the hem reached my ankles. The deep neckline of the thing was ornamented with frills, making it even more grotesque. It was like something a clown would wear.

We girls and women – shorn, disinfected, dressed in that absurd array of garments – were now permitted to locate the other members of our individual groups in a vast room at the front of the hall. How would we recognise each other? What could we rely on for identification? We had been reduced to the essence of ourselves, and we hoped we could discern the essence of those we were seeking. I picked out Marta from amongst the hundreds of faces; she was dressed in clothing as foolish as mine. And then Erna – terribly altered, and yet once I knew it was her, she seemed not altered at all. My mother found us, her three daughters, and from her mouth came a great howl of laughter that was also a heartbroken sob, drawn up from the depths of her being. Her three daughters – look at them! My mother's sobbing laughter infected us, and we howled too, a sound we had never before made in our lives. Others began laughing and sobbing simultaneously in just the same way, and in our hundreds we poured out our tears, the women and girls of Nyírbátor and its district, newly shorn at Auschwitz.

The guards didn't intervene to quell this mass hysteria. Perhaps they had witnessed the same thing in the past, and knew that the mad laughter would abate, which eventually it did. The shouted German commands then resumed. We were nudged and prodded and urged from the hall into a huge yard surrounded by tall wire fences. We rushed about in the yard, everyone hoping to find relatives. The hot May sun burned our naked skulls. We had not been told that we could not weep or call out for water, but we knew somehow that we must not. Five or six SS officers patrolled the perimeter of this crowd of hundreds, maybe even more than a thousand people. Some had dogs on leashes.

The rushing about in the yard died down; those who'd hoped to find sisters, aunts, nieces had either succeeded or accepted disappointment. I looked at my mother's face, below her bare skull. I was already becoming used to her new appearance. I saw the distress in her eyes but I also saw calm determination. I wasn't able to think, with the supreme conviction of times past, 'My mother will keep me from harm, always,' and yet I still held tight to the vestiges of that belief. Even in her ill-fitting attire, she radiated confidence.

At a little distance from where I stood in this dense crowd of frightened women and girls, a commotion had broken out – cries and shouts, wailing female voices. I stood on my tiptoes to see, but remained puzzled. My mother raised herself up as high as she could. 'It's the men,' she said, with a catch in her voice. 'They're bringing the men through.'

I pushed myself to the front of the crowd of women, pleading with God for a sight of my father. Behind the barbed wire were the men, all wearing striped, loose-fitting prison garments. And I saw him, my father in the striped pyjamas, on his face the dogged expression of a man who is suffering and who expects more to come. He was looking around, as all the men were, for a glimpse of a wife or daughter in the bizarrely dressed mass of shaven-headed women.

I called out to him: 'Daddy! Daddy!' He didn't turn his head. I screamed this time, 'Daddy!' and thrust my face towards him, only a couple of metres away. 'Daddy! Please! It's Baba!' This time he looked at me, but without recognition. I was, after all, so altered from the last time he'd seen me, hours earlier. I called with all the force of my lungs, 'Daddy! Daddy!' and something in my voice, something in the imploring look on my face, pierced his fear and despair and he saw that it was me.

For a few seconds he stared at me, and what was at first horror in his gaze – horror at the way I had been transformed into a rag-clad clown – changed to fatherly love and concern. Then he buried his face in his hands, and his shoulders shook with the rigour of his sobbing.

The sight of my father in his striped prison garb, his hands covering his face, was to be the last I had of him.

CHAPTER 13

The Feather Factory

Some amongst us guessed that we were in Poland. I had never before left Hungary, or not properly; in the days of freedom, I had travelled by train far enough north to have entered what had once been Slovakian territory. But it hardly mattered whether we were in Poland or Germany or any other country with a name we knew.

Beyond the tall wire fences lay what could have been farmland, although the paddocks were neither cultivated nor grazed. If this was Poland, it was rural Poland. The air, at least, should have smelt wholesome, but it was foul. It wasn't long before the inmates who had been at Auschwitz longer than us told us that those whom Mengele had sent to the other line were now being cremated. 'Were they shot?' someone asked. The answer was no: they were gassed to death. We were told this in a matter-of-fact way; the inmates, some of whom had been here for years, the 'block elders', were unsentimental. They had become seasoned witnesses to mass murder.

Those who had arrived in the same train with us, and who had seen people they loved being sent to the other line by Mengele, refused to believe what the inmates told us. But in time they came to believe it, just as I accepted that Mira, Mimi, little Kati and Klara, their mother, were dead and gone.

We were crammed into buildings that were designed to accommodate multitudes. Timber platforms – intended as bunks – ran down each side of a walkway of cement and bare earth that ran the full length of the building. Each platform had three levels and was about three metres wide; thirty-six people would sleep on each side. There was a gap of a metre or so between the sets of platforms, so that we could crawl onto the sleeping surface from either end. We huddled tightly together, not only through necessity but also for the sake of warmth. If you ended up in the middle of a row of twelve bodies, you faced a predicament if you needed to get to the latrines. One thousand, two-hundred and fifty women and girls were housed in each of these barn-like sheds.

When I first saw the interior of these sheds, and understood how closely we were to be packed in, I thought, 'No, this isn't possible.' Others, by their expressions, were thinking the same thing. Then I recalled the conditions in the cattle wagons that had brought us here and I knew that there was no mistake; what we would endure in the sheds was perfectly consistent with conditions on the train.

A human being, especially one who has known comfort and kindness in the past, finds it a difficult thing to accept that other human beings can be blind to suffering. If you are despised and abused, it is natural to ask yourself why. Had I ever treated anyone in the way they were treating me? Had I ever left myself open to revenge? I had not. And yet my mother and sisters and I, and the hundreds of other women in the shed, accepted what was done to us promptly enough. For reasons that no Jew has ever properly comprehended, we were despised. We accepted it.

The sheds were much bigger than an animal barn, and more crowded. Up high, near the gables, some windows were visible. Although dirty, these let in a dingy light during the day. Wooden posts rose from the floor, supporting the roof. Along the centre of the walkway dividing the platforms ran a low brick wall, the height of a seat. What function this served I never knew.

The shed was fitted with broad doors at one end, and these were thrown open during the day. When evening came the building was filled with the chatter of more than a thousand women and girls, subdued talk which lasted no longer than it took us to crawl onto our platforms and settle closely together. A block elder would sometimes stalk up and down the walkway while we settled. There were not so many guards, but we didn't even fantasise about running away. Auschwitz was a prison of a particularly vile sort, but beyond the tall, electrified wire fences was the much vaster prison of Poland. There was no escape. (It was said, however, that Jews who were sent to work outside the wire would occasionally find a way to disappear into the forest.)

Usually I slept on my platform with my body pressing against that of my mother and sisters. Sometimes I was next to other women. All social distinctions had been annihilated. The equality of the oppressed made us kind to each other. We ceased to bother about the fine discriminations people make when they live in comfort.

We were counted every morning. We stood in long lines out in the open, maintaining our groups of five. All of us still wore the garments we'd been given after we were disinfected and shorn. I was able to recognise others as much by their clothing as their faces. The roll call was indicative of the orderliness of the Nazis. They hated chaos and it was their great priority to avoid it. We were not tattooed with numbers, as victims at other times and places were, which perhaps suggested that by mid 1944 the Germans' rigid system was beginning to break down. The mass transportation of Hungary's Jews had come all at once: many thousands of people over a period of four months. Our group of five numbered off: Boeske, Erna, Baba and Marta Keimovits, and Annushka Zeger. Annushka was the quietest of the five of us, her head always bowed, shy even here where all shyness had been abandoned.

After the counting, we were fed. Breakfast amounted to no more than a small slice of black bread, smeared with some version of margarine. None of us would have eaten this bread in the days and years before we came to Auschwitz. But there, who could disdain food of any sort? The bread was doled out in the mornings by *stubendiensten*, a German word meaning 'room maids'. Each shed had its own *stubendienst*, and all were Polish prisoners of long standing. Of all the Jews in the camp, these Polish women were the most wretched, for they had seen so much suffering and death, and had been so often forced to accept that they could change nothing, ever, that they had become unfeeling. Our *stubendienst* had survived at Auschwitz for five years. Once in our shed I heard her answering an urgent, whispered question from a woman: 'Where in the camp are my sister's children?' The *stubendienst* jerked her head in the direction of the crematoriums. 'Up the chimney,' she said in a voice without any inflection.

In the evening we were fed again – a vile brown liquid that stank, and tasted even worse than it smelt. Each of us had her own metal dish and spoon, part of the parcels of possessions we'd brought with us to Auschwitz. One of the properties of this brown stuff was that, once you'd swallowed it down, you felt more famished than before. The sound all around in our shed was of metal spoons clattering and scraping against plates. As disgusting as it was, though, not a drop of food was left behind. The most persistent in our group at cleaning her bowl was little Annushka, who looked for a final tiny drop even when her plate was as clean as if washed. The poor child couldn't help herself. It was as if the action of bringing the spoon to her mouth consoled her somehow. Pampered as she had been in her life back in Nyír-bátor, she never seemed to fully understand the situation she was in. My mother pitied her, as did I, and watched her obsessive scraping of her bowl with pain and concern.

The idea behind preserving the able-bodied and the unencumbered from the gas chamber was that they would be available for various sorts of forced labour. The particular tasks depended on what needed doing. My mother, sisters and I were ordered to work in the feather factory. All the bedding that had been brought to the camp by the Jewish captives – cushions, doonas, pillows – was confiscated on arrival and delivered to a big warehouse, where we tore the covers open and emptied the feathers into big wooden containers. I expect that the feathers were used as filling for quilted cold-weather military coats.

There were few places at Auschwitz where we could put our hands on something that would ease the burden of captivity, but the feather factory was one. We were able to make aprons of the cotton or calico covers of the pillows and doonas by tearing or cutting them to shape, then we would wear them back to our shed. We would also take scissors from the feather factory, hidden in the folds of our garments. The next step was to fashion headscarves from the aprons. In the early mornings, when we were counted, the chill in the air was intense, and some women would trade a thin slice of their morning ration of black bread for such a scarf. Many also wished to improve their appearance; this wasn't vanity so much as a desire to look more human.

At the time, I had no misgivings about trading what we made from the pillow covers for extra bread, but it was a selfish act. We saw a chance to improve our own chances of survival, and we took it.

On our second day in the feather factory, Erna found a Hebrew prayer book inside a pillowcase. She brought it back to our shed, full of excitement. The prayer book connected us to the life we had known in years past. It evoked Shabbat, and our Seders at Pesach, my father's prayers, the lighting of the candles. This prayer book became our great treasure and solace. Another find was a small, round dish with some dried gravy stuck to it. Why it should have been hidden amongst the pillows, I cannot say. I picked at the gravy with my fingers, and ate. It was delectable.

A few days later, one of us found a *challah* cover while we were at work in the feather factory. The cover was embroidered with the Hebrew blessing of the bread. This find raised our spirits further. My mother said, 'I'll make a bag of this cover. We will keep our bread in it, so our bread will be blessed, always.' My sister Marta kept the shreds of this bag, discovered in the feather factory of Auschwitz, until her death.

CHAPTER 14

Selection

All illnesses at Auschwitz were terminal. The guards watched us closely for signs of weakness. If you showed any symptoms of sickness, you would be separated from your group of five and taken to the gas chambers. We understood this: we had seen women taken away to be killed and cremated. We knew that we mustn't cough too loudly, or falter when we were being counted in the early morning.

Even though I was perfectly aware of the likely consequences, one morning at the counting I fainted. I always knew when a fainting spell was imminent. I was standing in our group of five with my mother, Erna, Marta and Annushka. My mother and Erna, dreading what would happen if I fell to the ground, pressed close to me on each side and held me upright until I regained consciousness, and so I was spared. For that brief period of unconsciousness, I was not at Auschwitz but in some blissful realm with the sun shining. It was a jolt to awake to the bitter cold, to the sight of the assembled women in their ragged garments, and to hear my mother whispering urgently: 'Baba, wake up!'

New trainloads of prisoners arrived in their everyday clothes, their scalps unshorn. We saw them enter the camp. They stared at us through the electrified wire fence: some were visibly horrified at what they saw, some baffled. They did not know that they were looking at themselves a day into the future. We gazed back at them, feeling a type of pity. A day later, when we met these newcomers in the sheds and at the morning count, their heads bare, their clothing replaced by the same rags we wore, they seemed abashed. One of the new women said to my mother, 'When we saw you through the wire, we thought you were all lunatics kept separate from normal folk. That's what you looked like to us – lunatics, with your big eyes in your faces staring at us. And we thought: "See, they keep these mad women alive, so they will surely not kill sane people like us!"'

Always present in the air was the reek of human flesh being cremated. Ten days of breathing in that smell made me feel that it would be with me forever, even if I lived for another hundred years. The black smoke rose from the chimney stacks into the Polish sky. I didn't focus on the smoke; no one did. It quickly lost its power to shock or appal, and was just something that was happening – that was all.

We kept the black bread we were given in the morning in the bag my mother had made from the *challah* cover we had found.

We ate it during the day. We cared for each other. If one of us was given more bread than another, she would protest that she had been given too much. All of us kept a close watch on little Annushka, who seemed so frail. Not all families in the camp were as devoted to each other, and I witnessed some bitter arguments. But it came naturally to us to care for each other, even if the most we could do was share an extra morsel of black bread.

Mengele came to our shed, in his impeccable uniform and his polished boots. He stood on the walkway with SS guards on either side. He looked just as cheerful as when I first saw him on our arrival at the camp. One of the guards called for silence, and in an instant every murmur ceased. The women and girls on the platforms listened intently, although no one expected to hear anything good. Mengele spoke in German, and what he said was translated into Hungarian by a man in a uniform different to that of the SS soldiers.

'Has anyone here had a baby taken away?' the translator said. 'Now the mother can join her child to suckle her. Speak up.'

If any mother had been separated from her baby on arrival at Auschwitz, we knew, that baby would now be dead. What did Mengele want the mother for? Perhaps some mistake had been made, because normally a mother would not be separated from her baby; both mother and infant would be sent to the gas chambers. But we did not know about the 'experiments' Mengele was conducting in his Auschwitz surgery. He must have required the mother for some reason.

The beautiful Magda Reiner spoke up. 'Yes, my baby was taken from me,' she said. She must have known that she would die, but she did not want to go on living without her child. Magda was from Nyírbátor, and still a young woman. She made her way to the walkway, much to the satisfaction of Mengele, to judge from his expression.

I gazed at Magda with pity, but with admiration too. Her face was impassive.

The most terrifying of all the experiences we endured at Auschwitz were the regular 'selections', when all the women and girls in our part of the camp were compelled to show themselves naked to the inspecting SS officers. They were looking for symptoms of disease, or weakness, or anything that might restrict a prisoner in her role as a slave. To stand unclothed before the merciless gaze of the SS officers was humiliating, but we all knew that those judged ill or weak would be escorted to the gas chambers. A rash on the skin was enough to have you taken away. A cough. Even a dull look in your eyes or a stooped posture.

We stood erect, opening our eyes wide. An SS officer wearing an expression of mild disgust or sometimes boredom would stop before each of us and look us up and down. He would lean closer if he saw something that needed closer inspection: an abrasion, trembling lips, beads of sweat on the forehead that might suggest a fever. The smallest sign of infirmity was enough, since it was the intention of the SS to kill us all in time.

Often there was a struggle when the officers sent a woman

to the line of those who would die. She herself might refuse to go, or her family members might scream in horror and try to pull their relation back. There were never any reprieves. The officers would signal to the soldiers, and the soldiers would roughly separate the woman or girl from the others in her group and drag her away, naked as she was. She would remain naked in the line of selected women, and within a short time would be shuffling towards the doors of the gas chambers. We who had not been selected watched in pity, but perhaps also with a feeling of relief that the woman was not our sister, mother or daughter.

I prayed that my mother, my sisters and Annushka would remain strong and free from disease. But at a selection three weeks after we arrived at Auschwitz, Marta was sent to the line of those destined for the gas chamber. She must have looked too young for hard labour. My mother, Erna and I whispered together in a panic. The group to which Marta had been sent comprised older women and other young girls of Marta's age. Someone must go with Marta, we decided.

'Me,' I said. 'I'll go with her. I won't let her go alone.'

But as I was uttering those words, Marta herself tapped me on the shoulder. 'Go nowhere, Baba,' she whispered. 'I am here.' She had seen a chance when the guards were not looking and darted back to her mother and sisters. I reached out and took her hand. We waited in silence while the SS officers completed their selection. And we watched as the selected women were torn away from their families, screaming, resisting. That Marta was not amongst them was the joy of our silence. But of course there was no such relief for many other mothers and sisters.

When selection was over, we resumed our daily existence. We ate bread from our bread bag; we held the hand of a sister or mother; we checked each other for signs of illness; we talked. Sometimes we even laughed. I met girls from other parts of Hungary who had interesting stories to tell of their regions, their towns. We would chat about our lives before Auschwitz. I had as much to say as anyone. I told girls my age about the movies I'd seen, the books I'd read, the dresses I'd owned, the boys I'd fancied. It was the same for the other girls.

Sometimes we sat together and sang songs we'd heard on the radio back home – often quite cheerful songs. Even at Auschwitz, we wished to sing. Human beings can feel pain and hunger and terrible fear, but we must also give vent to our feelings of joy.

CHAPTER 15

Stutthof

After we'd been at Auschwitz for five weeks, my body had become used to the bunks of our shed. It was now no great chore to fall asleep on any flat surface. There was only one window in the entire building, high up, and I gazed through it before I went to sleep. The night sky over Auschwitz was always filled with stars.

As I looked up, I whispered the words of a Hungarian poem, a great favourite of mine. It was called 'From Soul to Soul', and the poet was Árpád Tóth.

> I stand by my window late at night,
> And through endless vistas, from afar,
> Into my eyes I collect the rays
> Of a remote, pale and trembling star.

From a million leagues this light has come,
Through icy, barren and the bare
Darknesses undeterred. For how long?
Who knows how many thousand years?

At last the old message has found me,
My eyes were its perpetual aim.
Content, it dies there; my tired eyelids
Cover it like a shroud on a coffin.

I once learnt that by screening through
The scientists' finest crystal instruments,
These lights from above bring us tidings
Of innate kinships, fraternal elements.

I close it into myself, drink it into my blood,
And secretly observe, listening, attending:
What ancient grief cries from light to blood,
From heaven to earth, from element to element?

Is the star sad and hurt because it is lonely,
Scattered as we are, orphans of the cosmos?
And because we shall never meet, never,
Through the night, the ice, the limitless reaches?

Oh star, do not cry! You're not more distant
Than are the terrestrial hearts here on earth.
Is Sirius farther or my friends and neighbours?
Who can tell, who can tell?

Oh, weep for friendship, weep and grieve for true love,
And cry over the path that leads from soul to soul;
We send one another feeble rays from our eyes,
And between us dwells an unfathomed, icy void.

One morning we were assembled and packed into open cattle wagons. They were to take us to a railway station – this was revealed to us by Jews who had been given positions of authority within the camp, the feared and despised 'kapos'. Our true destination, we were told, was Danzig – a port known to the Poles as Gdańsk. 'Then you will go across the water by boat,' the kapos said, 'maybe to Germany.' Despite everything, I was excited. I was to behold the sea for the first time in my life!

Other trains passed us on railway lines that ran parallel to the ones on which our train was travelling. We saw the passengers on those trains – normal citizens, men, women and children – and they saw us. I did not notice a single appalled expression. They were smiling, chatting to each other, reading newspapers and magazines, as if the war were a mere fairy story. How it hurt me to see these free and cheerful people. They did not care about us: that was what so wounded me.

At the waterfront in Danzig we climbed down from the carriages and were herded onto boats, below deck. Of the sea I noticed nothing at all. The journey had exhausted me and I fell asleep amidst the huddled mass of fellow prisoners, and I slept all the way to the port of our destination: Stutthof. We were marched through farming country to the town's concentration camp, a vast array of timber buildings enclosed by tall, barbed-wire fences, like those at Auschwitz.

The sight of the Stutthof camp was not quite as forbidding as Auschwitz, although it should have been. It was a death camp where at least eighty-five thousand people died from 1939 onwards, either murdered or after succumbing to hunger or illness. Auschwitz had shown us how far the Nazis would go to deal with their 'Jewish problem': they were prepared to commit mass murder. We had endured this shock already, and could not be shocked again.

Once again, we were housed in big timber sheds, only this time the sleeping platforms accommodated only four to a bunk. The food was better at Stutthof – we were given actual soup. But the 'latrines' were no more than lengths of timber above ditches.

A certain Magda, whose family name I never knew, was amongst the women in our shed. She was pretty but quite uneducated, and happy to indulge the Polish kapo, Max. He was tall, fair-haired, good-looking and vicious, and he fell in love with Magda. She would go off with Max to make love. Since Magda enjoyed the affections of the kapo, she was treated with deference by the rest of us, and it delighted her. She reigned in our shed as a queen. If you wished to stay in Max's good books, you were courteous to Magda, as he had the authority to punish prisoners, and to give or withhold favours. Max genuinely wished to please Magda, as if her consent was important to him.

Erna and I paid close attention to Magda – with smiles and flattery – in the hope of persuading Max to appoint us as *stubendiensten*. We had no great revulsion for Max. We discerned in him a number of unpleasant features, but we saw him as a resource that could be crucial to our survival.

And after a short time we did become *stubendiensten*. My chores in this role were restricted to serving the meal in the evenings. The soup was carried to our shed in a big black cauldron. We stood beside it while long rows of women waited with their bowls. I ladled an equal quantity of the soup into each bowl, painstaking in my efforts to ensure that no woman could complain that she had received less than her share. In the eyes of those girls and women I knew in Nyírbátor, and who knew me, there was always an imploring look: *Baba, it's me, from Nyírbátor – please, a little more.* But if I went along with such appeals, the soup would have run out before everyone was fed.

A *stubendienst* was in a position to feed herself a little more than the stipulated quantity of soup, and Erna and I both did. We fed our mother and Marta and Annushka more too. It was one of the benefits of the job. Those who had been denied extra would certainly have known that I did not deny myself or my family members; indeed, they would have been shocked if they thought Erna and I had forgone that privilege.

Within two weeks of our arrival at Stutthof we were joined by a number of Lithuanian women, all of whom were in a more wretched state than we Hungarians. Since 1940 the Jews of Lithuania had endured savage persecution by both the Nazis and the Lithuanians themselves. Most of the Lithuanian Jewish community of two hundred and eight thousand were murdered; by the end of the war, only thirteen thousand survived.

The new arrivals told us that the non-Jewish Lithuanians had been willing and enthusiastic deputies of the Nazis, accepting the task of murdering Jews without the slightest demurral. Usually this was done in village or town squares; the victims were shot in such a way that they fell into pits which they themselves had dug. Another method was to crowd Jews into a synagogue or barn, which was then set alight. Tales were also told of some few Lithuanians of great courage who had refused to join in the massacres, and were themselves shot or hanged. What the Lithuanian Jewish women had seen and suffered went beyond anything we had faced before 1944, and it showed in their faces. Their community had been one of the most vibrant and learned in Europe before the war. I pitied these women deeply. I didn't weep for them; none of us did. But I knew that they had experienced the most dreadful suffering.

It does not take much to kill a human being. One tiny microbe can do it, once it multiplies. A scratch that becomes infected. But it is just as true to say that it takes a great deal to kill a human being. Starved, exhausted, sick, we can yet survive. Most of the women and girls at Stutthof – and, no doubt, most of the men – were sick enough and starved enough and exhausted enough to have died, but we didn't, not unless we were murdered. My sisters and our mother didn't know where our father was, or whether he was alive or dead. We knew that Grandfather Ignac was dead. Our hearts were broken, but we held on to life.

Six weeks we survived in Stuthoff. In that time I sometimes experienced moments of complete blankness, of thinking nothing. Then a day came when we heard that we were to be sent to another camp. We didn't know why. News never reached us of the progress of the war, but this was the time when the Russians were advancing rapidly from the east. By early September 1944 the Germans were making a steady retreat, and Stutthof lay in the path of the Russian push towards Danzig. All we knew was that fifteen hundred of us were to be marched south, to somewhere in Poland. The SS must have wanted to keep us alive as slave labour.

Our destination, it was said, was to be a small town by the name of Baumgarten. Over the centuries, many Germans had settled in the region of our imprisonment, and quite a few towns had German names. So it was to Baumgarten that we marched, a slave army of Hungarian and Lithuanian women, guarded by twelve SS soldiers, a couple of them officers. They walked with us, some at the front, some on either side, a couple at the back.

The autumn weather was mild; the sun shone through the morning mist. The meadows were thriving with the lush grasses of the summer that had passed, and wildflowers of many colours grew everywhere. My mother was enchanted – she could never exhaust her love of greenery and fresh blooms, even in her starved state.

As we crossed the meadows, I noticed a friend of mine from Nyírbátor behaving oddly. She had become mentally unbalanced while we were at Auschwitz, the result of all that she had endured before she came to the camp and in the camp itself. My friend, a beautiful young woman, had been horribly abused, forced to cater to the lust of German soldiers. And now she had gone mad. Most days she could cope to a degree, with our help, but on this day something had given way in her mind. She sat down amongst the wildflowers, picking them, studying them fondly, singing to them. The great danger was that the soldiers would notice her, conclude that she was of no further use to anyone and shoot her.

I was anxious but I went to her, knelt and spoke soothingly: 'Yes, the flowers are pretty but we must keep walking ... We must, so stand up now, come along, take some flowers with you ...' The expression on my friend's face was like that of a child, and yet in her eyes I could still detect all that haunted her. She continued with us, but at the next selection she, her two sisters and their mother were taken back to Auschwitz.

After two days on the road we reached Baumgarten. Tents had been set up in a field to accommodate us – ten women to a tent. Before we settled for the night, we were instructed by the SS to clear an area of cow dung. This cleared area was to be the site of the kitchen. One of the officers, Oberschütze Huppert, made it known that he wanted five of us at the site early in the morning to set up the kitchen.

We settled into our tents for the night, two rows of five, body to body, with no more than rags to cover us. We were exhausted after walking for two entire days. As I prepared for sleep, I saw that Erna was keeping her eyes wide open. 'Erna, take your rest,' I whispered.

'Don't worry about me, Baba,' she said. 'Close your eyes.'

I did, and slept deeply. I woke just before dawn, feeling some movement beside me. It was Erna: she had remained awake all night in order to be the first one at the kitchen. She wanted the kitchen job so that she could secure extra rations for her family. She went off without a word and was the first to meet Oberschütze Huppert at the kitchen site. She impressed him with her zeal and became a favourite of his from that morning on.

CHAPTER 16

The Slave Army

The work the Germans had in mind for us was digging, and what they wanted dug were trenches. Some had to be about a metre deep, with the turf of the top layer piled on the lip of the ditch in small squares. From these trenches the retreating German soldiers would fire at the Russians as they advanced. We also had to dig some deeper trenches, about two metres, which it was hoped would block the Russian tanks. We were given shovels and mattocks, told what type of trench was required, and ordered to begin work.

The digging was arduous, and it went on all day, without respite. The earth was hard. Winter was coming and the moisture in the soil was beginning to freeze. Scarcely any rations were provided for us but we were expected to labour away without complaint. Some poor women could barely raise their mattocks to strike the earth, but they had to find the strength to keep at it all day. The SS stood over us and called out, '*Schneller, schneller*' – faster, faster. They separated the weak and ailing from the rest and took them away. Those of us who were a little stronger encouraged the weak to persist.

We received our breakfast before we started work for the day: black coffee from the dregs, and black bread made from grain husks. After that we got nothing until late in the afternoon, when we trudged back to the camp. Erna, in her role as kitchen maid, now slept near the site of the kitchen. Oberschütze Huppert allowed her to take a small container of extra food back to us, for which we were profoundly grateful. We did not eat this extra food in front of the others but in secret. Oberschütze Huppert was quite solicitous of the wellbeing of Erna and her family: he sometimes even asked if she had remembered to set aside extra rations for her mother. Erna also heated bricks and placed them in our bedding to warm our frozen toes.

After six weeks digging ditches in Baumgarten, we were told to pack up and assemble. Then we resumed our journey south, again on foot. The strategy behind our move from Stutthof to Baumgarten only became evident with the passing of time. We were in northern Poland, on the eastern side of the great Vistula River. The Germans must have hoped that the river would hold up the advance of the Red Army, and that the ditches we were digging would be a further barrier. But the German plan to survive by digging trenches in northern Poland was desperate; no army with the thirst for revenge that the Russians had developed over four years of fighting the Germans was likely to stop its pursuit.

Our march south took us to a new camp outside the village of Malchof. Of the village itself, we saw little – a glimpse of homesteads across the fields; the belltower of a small church. Once again we were accommodated in tents, and once again Erna lived at the site of the kitchen, still enjoying the goodwill of Oberschütze Huppert. We were now well into September of 1944, and the nights and mornings were piercingly cold.

By this time our work as ditch-diggers was visible in the skin of our hands, which were worn and calloused, and so ingrained with dirt that it seemed impossible that they might ever be clean again. We had become so habituated to the life we were compelled to live – to the labour, to the scarce food, to the cold – that we could no longer think of the end of the war.

It must have been mid-November when we abandoned the camp at Malchof and marched further south to a camp outside the village of Fridendorf. The landscape remained the same: the pastures of the broad Vistula floodplain, farmhouses in the distance or sometimes closer. If civilians – Poles or ethnic Germans – ever saw us, they paid little attention. We were merely a part of the war, not in the least interesting. Wars had rolled over the plains of northern Poland for centuries.

At Fridendorf I became ill with a respiratory infection. My temperature shot up to thirty-nine degrees and I was despatched to the camp's hospital tent. It might sound odd, but our camp included a tent set aside for this purpose. The SS shot many prisoners who fell ill but they couldn't kill everyone: they needed us to dig their ditches. And in fact there was more to it than this. A familiarity had developed between the slave masters and the slaves. Our relationships weren't as anonymous as they had been in the early days; some humanity had crept in.

It was early December 1944 when I went to hospital, the depths of winter. Ten patients filled the tent, most suffering from illnesses that had their source in poor nutrition and fatigue, or respiratory conditions like mine. I was happy to be in the hospital, for the weather outside was dreadful – snow and icy winds – and the ground as hard as granite. Within the tent, a wood stove kept the temperature bearable. We never got any medication: you either lived or died. Food was brought to the tent twice a day, and I benefitted from the extra rations that Erna sent from the field kitchen.

In order to remain in the hospital, though, my temperature had to exceed 'normal', or thirty-seven degrees. After a short time my fever disappeared and it became necessary to resort to trickery. When a thermometer was placed under my armpit, I would wait until the medical attendant turned to another patient, then I'd remove it and rub it vigorously against my bedding until the silver thread rose. Then I'd put it back under my armpit. The attendant would return, study the thermometer and say, 'Okay, you have to stay here for another day.'

Another benefit of being ill and confined to bed was the

opportunity it gave me to daydream with my friend Csopi, who was about my age. We spoke with longing of the day we would be free. We fantasised about our first ball gowns: what they would look like, the material they would be made from, the colour (green for me, pink for Csopi).

There was a Lithuanian girl, younger than me and Csopi, who languished in a bunk below us. We never paid much attention to her; we were so involved with ourselves and our daydreams. One evening we heard her talking to herself in Yiddish, and we leaned over the side of our bunk to listen more closely. 'The lice are leaving my head voluntarily,' she said. 'Look, they're going. Leaving my hair. Leaving my body.' Her eyes were wide open and staring, and she touched her hair with quick, picking motions. Csopi whispered to me: 'She's going to die.'

In the morning my mother came to visit me, and she saw immediately that the poor girl was dead. 'She has gone,' she said. Crouching beside the small body, my mother released a deep sigh and spoke a few words of a *viduy*. It is a *mitzvah* to speak such a prayer before your own death, and a *mitzvah*, too, if you help another with a *viduy*.

My mother resolved that this unhappy child should be given a proper burial. But the ground was frozen. She fetched a bucket of hot water from the kitchen, thawed a small patch of ground and scooped out a layer of earth with a strip of metal. Then she fetched more hot water, thawed another layer and excavated deeper. She continued until she was satisfied that the child could be decently laid to rest. My mother told me later that when she carried the girl's body to the grave, her limbs were still supple, her flesh soft. And she weighed no more than a cat, she was so thin.

It was in hospital that I discovered something that very few people in the world have ever known: absolute proof of the existence of a benevolent God. One morning I was told by a medical attendant that it was snowing heavily outside – a blizzard. I thought of my mother and Marta and Annushka slaving away with their tools in the bitter cold, and of all the other women, and I whispered this prayer to God: 'If You are God and You hear this, make the SS cancel work for today. Make the SS see that people cannot labour in such conditions, please, I beg of You. If You make this happen, I will believe – I promise, I will believe in You!' Then, within minutes of my prayer, Marta came to the hospital tent to tell me that the SS had cancelled the digging for that day. I was overjoyed, and my faith, which had faded a few years earlier under intellectual scrutiny, returned to me.

Thus I was in hospital on my seventeenth birthday. One year earlier, at home in Nyírbátor, I had been pampered and given presents. This year the day was as special for me as my mother and sisters could make it. They came to visit me in the hospital tent. My mother gave me a gold coin, a Napoleon, that she had found sewn to a coat she'd been given at Auschwitz. The coin had been covered in fabric and made to resemble a button. My mother, sensing there was something underneath the fabric, had picked the cloth away and found the hidden treasure. I had nowhere to spend the coin and would have to conceal it all over again, but my mother wanted me to have something that day, as a token of her love and perhaps also as a promise of better times to come.

After four and a half weeks, my phoney fever had run its course and I was sent back to join the slave army. Snow lay thick on the ground, and the wind was torture. I got ready to go with my mother and Marta and Annushka to the site of the digging. It was the nineteenth of January, 1945, a Friday.

That morning, the 'head girls' chosen by the SS to carry out various tasks hurried around saying that the guards wanted us to assemble immediately: we would be leaving the camp. No reason was given for the evacuation. We hurried to assemble, speculating what it might mean. *The Russians are coming... Germany has been defeated ... We are all to be killed and buried ... We are going to Germany ...*

As it turned out, one of the reasons for the assembly was to weed out those too weak to travel; they would remain in the camp. A number of women and girls were suffering horribly from boils on their flesh, and from chilblains that had compounded into something that would have required surgical treatment. Others were so malnourished that they could walk no more than a few steps. The women left behind would be shot; we were in no doubt about that. Some accepted their approaching death with equanimity; others felt wretched that what little life was left in their bodies was to be snuffed out. And, of course, for many there was the torment of leaving family members behind. As it turned out, some of the stronger ones with ailing daughters or sisters decided to stay behind and die.

My friend Csopi had a sister a year older than her, a timid and hesitant girl named Barbara. She was quite ill at the time of the assembly, and in pain from chilblains. She had made up her mind to stay at the camp and accept death. She begged her sister to remain with her. Csopi didn't want to die and didn't want to part from me, and somehow she persuaded Barbara to attempt the march to wherever we were going.

Another young woman I admired was Dora Cohen, who came from Kaunas, in Lithuania. She was a woman of great warmth and had a luminous intelligence. We all loved Dora; even the SS appreciated that she was an extraordinary person, and respected her. On that Friday morning, when news of the evacuation spread through the camp, Dora was ill – she had one of the many sicknesses that you can suffer when you are mal-nourished. So Dora was not amongst those who assembled for the evacuation, and we who knew her well were distraught.

Some years later, in Israel, I was taking a bachelor friend of mine to meet a cousin I hoped he might marry. I saw a well-dressed woman coming towards me on the footpath, and I recognised her. I was thunderstruck. 'Dora, dear God!' I cried. We laughed and kissed, then we introduced our companions and chatted a while. 'When we were left behind, we were waiting to die,' Dora said.

'But the guards did not stay – the SS abandoned us. And then a few days later the Russians came, and they treated us very well.'

We were told to form a column, five abreast, for the evacuation of the camp. We had no possessions, of course, other than a bowl, a spoon and a lice-ridden blanket each. We wore our blankets for warmth, arranging them on our bodies like coats. We also took our most precious items: the *challah* cover that my mother had fashioned into a bag, and inside it the bread we'd saved. The guards did not give us food; clearly they had made no plans for that as the evacuation had been too sudden.

It was winter in Poland, and the wind cut us to the bone as we marched. We wore wooden clogs, without socks. The snow hardened on the wood, creating a wedge, and often we slipped and fell onto the frozen ground. We helped one another up. 'Girls, try to keep your feet,' our mother said. 'Keep walking.' We all knew that the SS would haul us aside and shoot us if they saw us fall. Every so often I found the will to look over my shoulder at Csopi and Barbara. Walking was an ordeal for me, so I couldn't imagine what Barbara was enduring with her chilblains.

It was the same with the other women: the stronger supported the weaker, and exhorted them to keep going. But not everyone could be saved. I looked back once and saw an SS guard holding a woman down while another soldier shot her in the head. Then the body was thrown to the side of the road. I felt sick. We passed many bodies lying on the roadside – executed women from groups ahead of ours.

On each side of the roads we walked, the dormant paddocks of winter stretched away, and farmhouses appeared every so often. In the freezing cold our rows often became muddled, and I had to scan around for sight of my mother, Marta and Erna. My mother never let me get too far from her, fortunately. At one point I looked around again for Csopi and Barbara and failed to spot them. This meant that they were now dead on the roadside. At some time during the previous half-hour, they had given up the struggle. Perhaps it was Barbara who fell – that would seem likely – and Csopi who had refused to go on without her sister. After meeting Dora Cohen in Tel Aviv, I suffered deep guilt over Csopi's death. I felt it was my fault, since I had encouraged her to join the evacuation.

Then Annushka disappeared – frail, timid Annushka Zeger, who had become part of our family. Amid the snow and the bitter cold, walking with our heads drawn into our shoulders, we had lost track of her. She had lost her spectacles a day or so earlier, and without them she was almost blind. We had to guide her, straighten her path when she began to meander. She knew she had become a burden, and I suspected she had sat down of her own accord and waited for an SS guard. Poor Annushka – I despair.

CHAPTER 17

Escape

We sometimes passed civilians on the roadside as we trudged along on our journey to nowhere. Some were curious, but most were indifferent. One day our wretchedness roused the pity of an onlooker, who thrust a container of soup into the hands of one of our number. The woman took it, but a fight broke out immediately as others descended on her like a flock of ravens. It was horrible to watch – all sense of solidarity cast aside. The disputed soup container fell to the frozen ground and spilt. The women who'd been fighting threw themselves down and licked the soup from the ground before it could freeze.

We spent our nights in hay barns commandeered by the SS along the route. We always had to squeeze in; there was never enough space. Fights often broke out: 'Why are you stealing my space? Why are you pushing?' I didn't listen, so far as I could avoid it. I was still grieving for Csopi and Barbara.

On the twenty-fifth of January, a Thursday, we turned west and crossed the Vistula River. At the head of our column of slaves strode an SS officer in his great-coat, the collar turned up for warmth. The river was frozen and we walked across its surface with careful steps. The ice shone like a mirror in the winter sunshine, and even in the midst of my distress – frozen to the bone, weak, famished almost to the point of madness – a part of me thrilled to the sight.

Across the river, the roads were packed with ethnic Germans and Poles escaping west, towards Germany. The Russians were advancing, and although they were still east of the Vistula, it was feared that their progress would be rapid. Both the Poles and Germans dreaded the Russians, I knew. The ethnic Germans of the region considered themselves German citizens, of course, so that helped to explain their panic, but the Poles regarded Russia as a historical enemy and wanted to find a home in the eastern regions of Germany. Horse-drawn carriages made up most of the traffic on the roads. Carts were piled high with belongings, and on top sat bewildered and frightened children. These fleeing people barely acknowledged us; our ragged appearance would have repelled them, but in any case they had their own troubles. This was a retreat, or even a rout: an entire population was on the move.

The soldiers of the regular German armed forces were retreating too, but they were not amongst us. All we saw of the mighty German war machine that had swept everything before it a few years earlier was the handful of SS guards trudging along with their prisoners. All along the route of our march, dead bodies lay stiffened by the cold. Some seemed curled up, as if sleeping; others had died more violently, their arms thrown wide and their eyes looking upwards in a frozen stare.

We came at last to a large estate that was to serve as our camp for the night. We were told that we would rest for the following day. I doubt there was any charity in this; the SS officer in charge of us may have wanted a rest himself. We were sent to sleep in a large barn. We slumped onto the straw, drawing it over us for warmth.

Many women were now no longer with us. Marta was ill and growing steadily weaker. I was desperately worried about her. What would be the use of my own survival if I spent all the years of my life mourning my sister? I prayed for Marta's life to be spared, and I silently exhorted Marta herself to keep fighting. It was in that barn that my mother first spoke of a plan of escape. She and Erna and a Lithuanian woman were whispering together, close to where I lay in the straw. It was only gradually that I grasped what was being proposed.

Erna was adamant that we must try to run away. 'If we keep marching, we will all die,' she said.

My sister was not a woman who experienced rushes of blood to the head. She was, in all situations, cool, calm and collected. And yet here she was endorsing a plan that seemed to me madness. I butted in to say my piece: 'Are you all out of your minds? Where would we go? And how?'

My mother, Erna and the Lithuanian clearly considered me unqualified to offer an opinion: their glance at me was brief, patient and dismissive. Then they went back to their planning. Offended, I huddled back into the straw, muttering to myself: 'They are crazy, mad! Where would we head? It's all enemy land!'

That night I was wakened by cries: 'Fire!' The SS guards were rousing us and ordering us to leave the warmth of the barn for the wintry cold outside. We stood shivering in the darkness while the fire was extinguished. Once back inside the barn and again covered in straw, my mother and Erna and the Lithuanian woman returned to their escape plans.

When daylight came we were not kept in the barn; we were permitted to look around. The homestead of the farm was some distance away, and I could just make out the farm workers going about their business. As Erna wandered about that morning she discovered the opening to an empty cellar. The floor of the cellar was concrete, and the space was divided into cubicles by metre-high concrete walls. Possibly it was for storing grain. Erna showed the cellar to my mother and the Lithuanian woman, and also to me, despite my scepticism.

My mother, who had the final say on everything, said that the cellar was as suitable a hiding place as we were likely to find. 'We'll do it,' she said. 'In the morning, before we start marching again, we'll come here and hide. When everyone has gone, we'll steal back to the road and return the way we came.' My mother hoped we would come upon the Russians and seek their protection.

The entire escape plan depended on us waking early the next morning, but we did not. The whole camp was in motion by the time we emerged from our warm nests in the straw. We gathered our few possessions and were about to join the rest of the women outside the barn when one of the SS guards, Sturmscharführer Augele, told my mother to move a straw bale, then turned his back and left the barn. My mother moved the bale, and as she did so whispered to us, 'Follow me – we're going to the cellar.'

We slipped out of the barn, skirting the area where the women who were about to begin the day's march were hurrying into formation, found the cellar and climbed down into it. We huddled together in one of the cubicles and prayed. Our prayer was the *Yevarechecha Hashem* blessing: 'May the Lord bless us and watch over us, may God show us favour and be gracious to us ...' We prayed over and over in that cubicle, huddled together.

When we finally ceased praying, we listened. Barely any light found its way into the cellar, and I could just make out the shadowed faces of my sisters and my mother, the glitter of their eyes. We heard not a single voice, not the slightest suggestion of movement, and so at last my mother opened the trapdoor and waited cautiously for a further few minutes.

'Come on,' she said. 'But quietly.'

Before we could move, we heard someone approaching. My mother closed the trapdoor hurriedly. It was opened again, this time by one of the Polish farm workers – not every Pole had fled

the Russians. He was perfectly sanguine about finding four ragged women sheltering in the cellar. He asked us in German what
the matter was: did we not realise that the other women had
departed? My mother answered that her youngest daughter was
stricken with illness and suffering from chilblains, and we'd been
resting here in the cellar.

Mother's story was absurd, but the fellow listened calmly,
without judgement. He advised us to make haste and catch up
with the others. He said that they were not so far ahead. 'I'll show
you which way to go,' he assured us. And so he did, still urging
us to hurry, as if he thought we were desperate to be reunited
with the other women. We had to play along: 'Thank you, thank
you so much.' After a while he left us and went to attend to his
work. We shuffled in the direction he'd indicated for a short time,
but when he was out of view my mother began looking for
another hiding place.

This was the first time in eight months that we had been
alone: no guards, no instructions, just four Hungarian women
on the run in northern Poland. The experience was frightening
but exhilarating.

We found a stable that appeared to be deserted; it was on the
grounds of the estate but distant from all the other buildings. A ladder rose from the floor to a loft. We climbed it and covered ourselves
with hay. Then we discussed our situation: what should we do
next? The front could not be far away. Return to our original plan
and walk back the way we'd come, into the arms of the Russians?

'Listen,' my mother said, 'between us and the Russians is the German army. We might meet up with the Germans before we find the Russians.'

'Then we should stay here, where we are,' said Erna. 'The Germans will pass by, heading west for their homeland. Then the Russians will come, and we'll show ourselves.'

'How long will that take?' I asked. 'How long can we stay alive here?'

'Here we're sheltered and warm,' Erna insisted. 'If we leave this stable, we might not find such a place again.'

Mother had a few scraps of bread left in her bag and a tiny amount of sugar that she'd scavenged from somewhere. We also had a small canteen filled with water; it was frozen, so we had to thaw it with our body heat when we wanted to wet our mouths. But even if we were somehow able to find the same amount of food and water each day, we would surely die from hunger. We had to hope that the Russians would quickly find us and free us.

We lay close to each other in our nest of hay, sleeping now and again, trading a few sentences, listening to every sound, judging it for some signal of relief on its way. There was, of course, little to hear: birdsong, the muffled throb of an aircraft passing high overhead, the breathing of my mother and sisters.

A day later the German army arrived and stabled their horses below us. We listened in silence to the racket of the soldiers as they settled their horses into the stalls, and to the stamping and neighing and snorting of the beasts. We exchanged glances of fear, and although we said not a word, I mouthed the message: 'We're trapped.'

My mother nodded, then beckoned for Marta and Erna and me to come closer. 'We'll wait,' she whispered. 'Surely they won't stay for long. They'll want to keep ahead of the Russians.'

Two more days passed, and still the horses and the soldiers could be heard below. We were by this time desperately hungry, and thirsty too. We'd exhausted our canteen of water, and we knew that another day up in the loft might finish us off.

'Erna, Baba, go down to the stable and show yourselves,' my mother whispered. 'If they kill us, then that is our fate. But we cannot stay up here and die without attempting something.'

We nodded. The plan was very risky, of course, in more ways than one. The soldiers were men, and we were women – bedraggled, but women nonetheless. But starvation encouraged us to take the risk. We shook off the hay, crawled to the ladder and began to descend. Glancing down, I saw amazed expressions on the upturned faces of the German soldiers. Soon Erna and I were standing on the floor of the stable, not knowing what look to adopt, or what to say.

One of the soldiers gazing at us was holding a wooden pail filled with water; he'd frozen in the act of offering it to the horses. Without a second's hesitation, I took two steps, raised the pail to my lips and drank deeply. The soldier kept hold of the pail and made no attempt to restrain me. When I had drunk my fill, Erna took my place and drank. The soldiers were grinning in a some-what foolish way, saying nothing.

I explained in German that we had been left behind by our companions, all women, who were heading west, and that one of our number, still up in the loft, was sick and unable to walk. The soldiers merely nodded and shrugged. They had little interest in the stories of two ragged young women. We were told to head west and see if we could catch up with our 'transport'; if we couldn't, perhaps we would find another that would take us to our 'destination'. We called to Mother and Marta to come down from the loft, and they drank too. We thanked the soldiers for the water and headed west – the direction in which the soldiers had pointed us. Once we were beyond the gates of the estate, however, we turned east.

We had escaped the slave army and the SS on the twenty-eighth of January, and it was now the fourth morning after, so it was on the first of February, 1945, that we went out through the estate gates. We walked down the road that had brought us here, scanning the fields left and right for a farmhouse that we might approach. Our temporary home in the hay of the loft began to seem more and more luxurious with every step we took, our faces against the bitter north-east wind blowing down from Siberia. The ground underfoot was frozen solid. Marta was suffering greatly, but did not complain.

At around midday Erna saw a farmhouse a way across a paddock, and we trudged towards it with a kind of hope. My mother went to the front door and knocked while Erna, Marta and I stood a little further back. The door was opened by a gaunt man in his fifties. From behind him peered a number of other faces, men and women. They were all Poles, to judge from their clothing, and the gaunt man confirmed this. We knew enough Polish by now to understand what he was saying: they were all refugees. 'Madam, there is no room here,' he said. 'We are a large number. I am sorry, but there is no room.'

'Could you at least spare some food?' my mother asked, but the man was reluctant to give away the food of the crowded household.

At this point I was mortified by my mother's behaviour. Had she turned into a beggar? She lifted her hands and stepped a little closer to the man at the door. 'Please give us just a few scraps – please, just a few scraps. These are my daughters, you can see how wretched they are ... For me I don't care, but the girls, sir, please ...'

The man relented and gave us some bread, which was soft and not stale. It tasted like food of the gods. We weren't given a whole loaf, but what those good people spared was enough to fortify us for the rest of the day.

CHAPTER 18

A Roof over Our Heads

Some of the fields we passed still had the remnants of crops that had been harvested in summer and autumn. We could see the bulbs of sugar beets in one field, so we uprooted them and stored them inside our clothing, against our chests. Once they had thawed, we chewed on them for sustenance.

We also had to find shelter. We were looking out for another barn that might have a bed of straw. The sun was shining but it didn't provide much warmth. Soon evening would come, and if we were still out in the open we would doubtless freeze. In the distance I saw the wooden buildings of a hamlet. 'Over there!' I cried. We took the track up to the buildings, but as we came closer we saw a group of German soldiers by the barn. We tried to slip by but it was too late: we'd been seen.

'Where are you going?' one of the soldiers called.

'We're searching for lodgings for the night,' my mother replied.

The soldier, who was not SS, did not seem hostile. 'Are you hungry?' he asked.

My mother paused. If we were to tell the soldier just how hungry we were, he might see that we were Jewish runaways. Most refugees from the fighting carried some bags with a few possessions; we had absolutely nothing. Nevertheless, my mother conceded that we were all hungry.

'Come in and have something to eat,' the soldier said. We followed him into the house, where a field kitchen had been set up for the soldiers. Four were sitting in the kitchen, enjoying warm soup, and they offered each of us a bowl.

I swallowed a spoonful of my soup – and fainted. Usually, my fainting spells had no physiological cause; they just came and went. This time, the warmth of the kitchen overwhelmed me. When I regained consciousness I was sitting on the bottom step of some stairs that led up from the kitchen; my mother was beside me, deep concern on her face. The soldier who'd invited us into the farmhouse was attempting to untie the string that was wound around my waist as a belt – it was holding my scrap of blanket in place – so that I might breathe more easily. My mother strove to prevent him from untying the string; the indelible red star on the back of my Auschwitz dress would immediately reveal me as a Jew. I also had some sugar beets thawing against my flesh.

Despite my mother's best efforts, the German soldier found the beets. 'Girl, what are you eating?' He was plainly distressed that I should be relying on the dirt-caked roots of beet for sustenance. I could see the concern on his face, and indeed on the faces of the other German soldiers. Unlikely as it seemed, these Germans had hearts.

They said we could work in their kitchen, peeling potatoes and things like that, and in return we would have shelter and protection. Also we would have a big bed in which to sleep, a bed with a mattress and blankets. The soldiers would sleep on the floor. We were happy to accept the hospitality of these German soldiers, but we realised we must always keep our red stars concealed. For the time being, we were simply four destitute women, not four destitute Jewish women.

One soldier by the name of Fritz was especially well mannered and kind. He spoke to us in a genial way and showed us respect. His consideration went so far as to worry about what would become of us when he and the other soldiers moved on, as they would within another day. The Russians were on the east bank of the Vistula, which was not far away. 'I'll find a place where you can stay,' Fritz said. 'Leave it to me.'

And he did indeed find lodgings for us. How pleased he was! He said he'd duped an old German-Polish couple into accommodating us. It was the duty of soldiers at that time to find lodgings for refugees they came across, and those householders who had space were obliged to accept anyone sent their way. Fritz delightedly told us that he'd given this old couple a choice between finding room for a mother and father with seven children and four horses, or for a mother with three daughters. 'You see how I made the choice easy for them?' he said. 'They looked at me sourly, not pleased that they had to shelter anyone at all, but they said, "We'll take the mother and her daughters." So now they will welcome you as the lesser of two evils!'

Fritz took us to our new hosts and introduced us. The couple were also looking after an uncle in his eighties, and they kept a younger man, a Ukrainian, as a sort of servant. Outdoors, three cows were stabled; indoors, the larder was full.

Subterfuge was necessary, of course. Our family name was a problem. The Poles of the household would find Keimovits suspect as a surname, as well as awkward to pronounce. After some consultation between ourselves, we came up with a new family name: Fleischmann, the name of one of our German SS guards. We also adopted Christian given names: I would be Margareta, Erna would become Sonya, while Marta would remain as Marta. Mother would simply be Frau Fleischmann. We didn't bother with a family back story, and it never came up in conversation.

We all thrived on the food we enjoyed at the home of our host family, but it was particularly important for Marta. Her chilblains did not heal completely, but at least they caused her less pain. Still, we were living in a virulently anti-Semitic household. When members of our host family started talking about '*verfluchte Juden*' ('cursed Jews'), we kept quiet. According to our hosts, it was the *verfluchte Juden* who came each day in their aeroplanes to bomb the countryside, and the *verfluchte Juden* who had made this war that had cost so many lives and caused so much hardship. The heroic German people had done all that they could to rid Europe of the *verfluchte Juden*, but not enough, apparently. The vilest of all was the old uncle, who ranted in this way constantly; our tasks were always accompanied by his Jew-hating speeches.

People came to the house every now and again – mostly neighbours stopping by for a few minutes to gossip. Some regarded us with suspicion. One of these visitors, a Polish woman, gave my mother a searching look and said in a low voice, 'I've seen a few runaways like you.' My mother did not reply, but I'd overheard and a chill crept over my body. The members of our host family didn't grasp what the Polish woman meant by 'runaways' and made no issue out of it. If they'd understood, they would probably have searched for an SS squad to take us away.

German soldiers came to the house too, the remnants of an army scattered by defeat at the Vistula. They told us their story, initially one of success in halting the Russian advance, but then of facing a reinforced attack, and ultimately of defeat, retreat and disarray. I thought of the many trenches we'd dug in the freezing weather, designed to halt this advance, and now those trenches were in the captured territory of the Red Army. The soldiers who came to the house begged for food, as we had, and they were ragged, as we were. But they were more demoralised than us. We had survived so much and were seasoned by suffering. The

German army was just in the early stages of the demoralisation it would endure over the next three months.

These ragged soldiers did not seem to suspect that we were escaped Jews. I doubt they would have cared, such was the state they were in. We sat with them at the kitchen table and watched them eat, and listened to their tales of battles and bloodshed. My mother spoke German to them. I would break slices of bread in half and give one part to a soldier, eating the other half myself. I didn't hate these poor, humiliated boys, and I listened to them with sympathy. I knew how it felt to be desperately hungry and defeated.

Considering the months we'd spent in arduous physical labour, I was fairly lucky to have escaped injury. Indeed, we had all avoided broken bones and serious cuts. We didn't avoid blisters and bruises, but those we could tolerate. One day I was sent out to fetch wood for the fire, and I slipped and fell heavily on the icy ground. I broke my fall with my hands, gashing my left wrist badly. I went inside holding my wrist and showed the wound to my mother. I recalled a girl I knew in one of the camps telling me of an injury her father suffered when his hand went through a pane of glass, cutting him so deeply that his nerves were severed; he had lost all sensation in his fingers from that time on. I was sure I would be left restricted in the same way. The wound was bathed and wrapped in a makeshift bandage, but it required expert attention. We were told that there was a German field hospital within walking distance.

My mother and I set off for the field hospital in the late afternoon. We knew that we were taking our lives in our hands, but our experiences as runaways had made us daring rather than fearful. Aircraft roared overhead as we walked through the snow; whenever we heard them thundering in for a strafing run, my mother and I hid in a ditch.

The field hospital was essentially for German battle casualties, of course, but the medical staff were prepared to treat the locals – more willingly if you were an ethnic German. And for the purposes of our visit, we were ethnic Germans. Mother did all the talking. 'My daughter has done herself some harm, as you can see. An unfortunate fall while running from the aeroplanes!' The doctor may or may not have believed her; he had enough to do without worrying about the veracity of tales brought to him by civilians. He called in a colleague, who administered a general anaesthetic, and I dissolved into blissful unconsciousness.

My mother sat by me while the doctor stitched me up. Her great anxiety, as she told me later, was that I would wake up and blurt out something in Hungarian. When I did come to, I said, in perfect German, '*Wo bin ich?*' ('Where am I?') My whole arm, from my fingers to my shoulder, was bandaged, as if I were indeed a casualty of the battlefield.

The irony of our situation at this time did not escape me. The Germans, after herding us into a death camp, and then forcing us to trudge like beasts all over the north of Poland, had now become our benefactors. It was the Germans who had fed us in their field kitchen when we were starving, it was Fritz who had found us our lodgings, and it was a German doctor who had ministered to my wound.

It was late in the evening when we left the field hospital and began our journey back to the farmhouse. The snow had ceased falling and the sky was clear. Overhead, countless stars glittered. My mother and I said little to each other. Once again, my mother's daring and wherewithal had found a solution to a problem. While she lived, she would make sure we lived.

CHAPTER 19

The Fleischmanns of Poland

My impression as a wandering former captive of the Germans was that the ethnic Germans of Poland had welcomed the Nazis as liberators, while a significant number of Poles, too, were happier with a German occupation than with the prospect of a Russian invasion. The ethnic German family who had been compelled to lodge us were amongst those who wanted to get out of Poland before the Russians arrived, and within days of my return from the field hospital, the husband and wife packed their bags and announced their departure. The old uncle and the young Ukrainian fellow were the only ones to stay behind.

They sternly advised us to evacuate as well, but since they were ultimately heading for Germany, we could not go with them. As an excuse, my mother said that my bandaged arm would never stand up to the rigour of the journey. The family was in too great a hurry to argue the point, and so it was agreed that we, the Fleischmanns, would remain behind in the house, milk the cows, care for the vile uncle and make whatever sort of deal with the Russians we could. One day, the family might return, and if that happened, we would hand back the keys to the house.

Thus we became the occupants of a farm in Poland, with three cows, various other beasts, a Ukrainian servant and a larder still fairly well stocked. The Fleischmanns were a lucky family. We still had the uncle on our hands, but by this time his diatribes were no more than background noise to us. We fed him and made sure he was comfortable, but we'd become inured to his ranting.

The house was directly in the path of the German retreat, and soldiers continued to come knocking at our door. We fed them; they were meek enough in defeat. One soldier I recall in particular. He was about twenty-five and had barely eaten for weeks, but he paused between mouthfuls of soup to ask me: 'Do you know that hunger is painful? It is actually painful.' And, having asked me, he returned to the soup.

The retreating soldiers became fewer as the days passed. We rose in the morning to milk the cows, and we waited for whatever was fated to come our way that day. It wasn't possible to fashion a sensible plan in the turmoil of the battlefield; having a place to live and food to eat was the best situation we could expect for the time being.

Just before dusk one day a group of six German soldiers came to the door asking for food. My mother showed them in and served them the hearty soup she kept on the stove for such arrivals. They were grateful, and the most senior of them advised us to evacuate and escape the approaching Russians. 'We are the last German soldiers you will see,' he said. 'The very last. After us, the Russians. I don't have to tell you what you should fear. You know. If the Americans were coming, you would have nothing to fear. But the Russians – be warned.' The soldiers departed and we were left with our fears. My mother remembered the reputation of the Russian soldiers in the Great War.

In the early days of March 1945, after we had been at the farmhouse about a month, the first signs of the approaching spring appeared. The ice and snow began to thaw, and the days were a little longer. The clouds that had brought the winter snow disappeared from the sky, and now and again the sun provided a little warmth. My wound was healing steadily; when the dressing was changed, there was no sign of infection taking hold.

Because I was an invalid, I had a single bed to myself, while Mother, Erna and Marta shared a double bed in the same room. One night I had a very vivid dream. The setting was an amphitheatre, huge, with tiered seating to accommodate thousands of devout Jews. The men were at prayer but I was standing in their midst, and what I was most aware of was their complete ignorance of my presence. I struggled to draw attention to myself, waving my arms about: 'Look at me, can you not see me?' The faces of the men in their prayer shawls were impassive, their gaze fixed on something distant. I was anxious and afraid, horribly disappointed that my efforts to draw some response all failed. I awoke bereft, and felt troubled in my soul.

That was a night of events. My dream was soon followed by the sound of strange voices in the house. We sat up in bed, and a minute later three soldiers entered our bedroom, their faces illuminated by lanterns. We stared at them in fright. They were not German soldiers; they were Russians.

The soldiers gazed at us, giving no hint by their expression what they were thinking. They had our Ukrainian with them. One soldier spoke rapidly to our man; he appeared to be telling him to lead the way into the next room. Was this to check if there were German soldiers hiding there? The soldier returned from the neighbouring room carrying a pile of papers that I immediately recognised as patterns for women's garments. He stood in the middle of the room and, rather melodramatically, tore them to pieces. His expression was one of accusation, and it occurred to me that he must have believed that these carefully drawn and detailed patterns were maps.

One of the soldiers stepped closer to my single bed and lifted the blanket that was covering me. I was terrified. At that moment the sound of a pistol shot echoed in the room, then loud, angry cries. It wasn't immediately possible to work out what had happened, but after a while it became clear that the soldier standing at the door had accidentally shot himself. He'd been holding the handle and trigger of a pistol in his back pocket, ready to draw it if he needed to, and had somehow jerked the trigger and shot his own backside. The wounded soldier cried out and hopped about in pain while his two comrades tried to help him. They finally succeeded in supporting him and took him away.

This first encounter with the Red Army left us shaken, and we remained in bed for the rest of the night. At six, my mother dressed and went to milk the cows, but Erna and Marta and I stayed where we were. We were very concerned that what the German soldiers had said about the Russian soldiers would prove true.

As if to confirm our fears, a soldier came into the bedroom, studied us one at a time, then told Marta to dress and follow him. Erna threw back her covers and leapt from bed to find our mother and tell her that Marta was in danger. The soldier hastened after her, leaving Marta behind. I got out of bed too, and Marta and I also ran in search of our mother. As we reached the kitchen, a sixteen-year-old Polish girl who came each morning to fetch milk for her family arrived. She was a very pretty girl, and the soldier changed his preference from Marta to her. He told the girl to follow him, and she had no choice but to do as she was told. Marta, trembling and terrified a minute earlier, wept with relief.

How many soldiers intended to use the house, and for how long they would stay, we didn't know. But what we did know was that we were all in danger. We couldn't expect to be saved every day by a clumsy soldier shooting himself, or by the sudden arrival of a pretty Polish girl. But to leave the house and take our chances in a region that would soon be swarming with Russian troops was foolhardy. Later that day, our mother gathered us in the kitchen and told us her plan. 'I will take you, Erna, and you, Marta, and hide you in the hayshed,' she began. 'I'll bring you food. Baba, you will stay here in the house with me. With your bandaged arm, none of the soldiers will want you.'

We agreed, but I doubt if any of us thought this a particularly brilliant plan. Surely the soldiers would sooner or later notice Mother going to the hayshed with food. And she herself, even at forty-four, was an attractive woman.

My mother concealed Erna and Marta in the hayshed. But as she was returning, a Russian soldier noticed her and his suspicions were aroused. He went to the shed to investigate and found my sisters. My mother and Erna and Marta all became frantic, pleading with the soldier to let them be. And the soldier was sympathetic: he made calming motions with his hands and led them to understand that he would do nothing against them.

From the kitchen I could hear the commotion, but of course I didn't know what was unfolding. It sounded awful, though, and I was distressed. In this state I suddenly found myself attempting to fend off another soldier, this one a crazy drunk, my bandaged arm not the least impediment to him. My struggles slowed him, though. He freed one arm and grasped his rifle, putting the muzzle to my forehead. He was shouting at me and I was shouting at him; neither of us knew what the other was saying, but at the same time we did. I was shrieking for help but also crying out a Jewish prayer, *Shema Yisrael*; as a child, I'd heard that this is the prayer of the dying. I wanted to be heard by God.

At this moment, my mother and sisters and the other Russian soldier burst into the kitchen. The soldier who had shown my mother and sisters such kindness now rushed at his comrade, quickly overpowering him, and seized the rifle. Then he took his comrade away, signalling to us to calm ourselves.

Within a few hours, more soldiers arrived. One took a particular interest in me and learned my name. I tried to keep my eyes averted, but whenever I looked up his gaze was on me. That night he came to our bedroom and leaned over me, whispering in broken German: 'Margareta, Margareta, let me get into bed with you … please, Margareta – four years of war, four years, and I have not been with a girl … I beg of you, Margareta, please …' I was silent. I don't know that I was even breathing. I pulled the blanket over my head and squeezed my eyes shut. The soldier's pleading went on and on, and I felt him pawing at the blanket. I thought: 'God save me, God save me.' And He did. The soldier gave up his importuning and stole away. But the sickness of dread stayed with me for hours, all through that sleepless night.

The soldiers packed up and departed, on their way to Germany. More soldiers would come to the house, I was certain. The memory of that drunken soldier became fixed in my mind. I had always been able to rely on my nerves, but I couldn't keep my nerve now. I was a wreck. I clawed at the walls with my fingers, and I clamped my hand over my mouth to stop myself from screaming. When I could bear it no longer, I told my mother what had happened. I had wanted to spare her the story of the

Russian soldier but it became too much for me. I just had to share my pain.

The old man was in bed; the Ukrainian was about his chores. The danger we faced now seemed as great as any we'd known. We had been saved by a soldier who knew the difference between right and wrong, and then by the power of my prayers. But we would not always be so fortunate.

'The cellar,' Mother said.

We knew of the existence of this cellar; we'd looked down into it a few times in the days before our host family had departed. Mother cleared the living room floor of rugs and lifted the trap-door to the cellar. An odour of mildew wafted up from the darkness. We had to overcome our strong feeling of repugnance, but Erna, Marta and I climbed down the ladder into the gloom. But better the gloom than falling into the hands of another drunken soldier. We could at least be thankful that it was now early April, and the weather was a little milder.

From inside the cellar, we heard a truck arrive: the grinding of gears, the slamming of doors. The boots of soldiers thudded on the floor above us – six or seven of them, possibly more. We heard their voices: one was telling my mother in German that the Red Army was requisitioning the house for the following day and night. 'For a day and a night?' she asked in disbelief. I could tell from the pause before she spoke how distressing this news was to her.

The soldier talking to my mother paced about while he was speaking. I heard his footfalls stop. He rapped the floor above us with the heel of his boot. 'What is below?' he said to my mother. She made no spoken reply. Maybe she was shaking her head, as if in ignorance of what the soldier was talking about. Then came the scraping of chairs being moved.

The soldier lifted the trapdoor. We could see him but he couldn't see us. He called for the Ukrainian and ordered him to climb down the steps. He may have been taking precautions in case German soldiers were hidden below. Once the Ukrainian was halfway down, the soldier descended. He shone a flashlight beam about until it settled on Marta, Erna and me, huddled together in fear. He told the Ukrainian to stay where he was, then called to us to come up the steps. We did as we were told.

My mother was standing tall in the kitchen, while the soldiers stood about looking puzzled but pleased. Four attractive women, all of a sudden! The officer took us to the room where the ill-tempered old man lay on his bed. 'Who's he?' he asked in German.

'A Pole,' my mother said. 'He was here when we came.'

'Came from where?' the officer asked.

She didn't answer. No doubt she was considering whether to reveal that we were Jews who had once been at Auschwitz. We girls looked to her for guidance. We had hidden our red stars so assiduously for all this time, and now, when it became safe to reveal them, caution stopped us from doing so.

'All right, sit down,' said the officer. He could see that my mother had something to say but would need coaxing.

We sat on the chairs and on the side of the bed of the old man, who stared at one then another of us with his customary malice. The officer told us in his basic German that he would have the Russian-speaking Ukrainian translate what he had to say to us, and he called the man into the room. We had to hope that he would translate what Mother said faithfully. We didn't trust him at all; he had kept himself aloof from us over the whole period of our time at the farmhouse. But maybe he would be too frightened to distort what was being said. As a Ukrainian, he had reason to feel in some danger: the Russians correctly considered the Ukrainians to have been collaborators with the Nazis.

The officer folded his arms and nodded at my mother. 'So tell me,' he said.

My mother began by declaring that we were Jews. 'Jews escaped from hell,' she said. 'For the Germans have been killing Jews in great numbers. We were sent to Auschwitz in the south, where many Jews were murdered, and also many Russian prisoners of war. Then the Germans sent some of us women here to the north to work for them.'

Once Mother had told part of our story, we felt free to chime in with details of our own, encouraged by the sympathetic expression on the face of the officer. We showed him the identification numbers on strips of fabric that we'd been ordered to sew on the sleeves of our garments back in Auschwitz – 37896, 37897, 37898 and 37899, as well as Annushka's number, 37900, which we had saved. And we displayed the red stars on the back of our Auschwitz dresses. The officer nodded at intervals and his growing understanding became apparent. Sometimes, instead of nodding, he shook his head, as if in shock and disbelief.

'On the road,' said Mother, 'many of us were shot. If we became sick, we were shot. If we stumbled, we were shot.' When she wished to demonstrate being shot, she raised an imaginary rifle to her shoulder.

The other Russian soldiers stood at the doorway, captivated. All of us grew excited as we talked. Not once since our expulsion from Nyírbátor had we been in a position to tell our story to a sympathetic listener, other than to those like us, who were enduring the same ordeal.

The Russians began talking too, and adopted my mother's demonstrative method of storytelling. They acted out their questions for us with gestures and dumb show. For some reason the whole business was highly animating: together we were constructing a complicated story without a common language.

One word common to both the Russians and to us was 'Fritz' – the stereotypical name for any German, just as 'Ivan' was the de facto name for any Russian. We had somehow come to believe that another word the Russians used repeatedly – *voyna* – meant 'hungry'. Actually, it meant 'war'; God knows how we so mangled the meaning. At one point in the chaotic exchange my mother said, '*Fritz voyna! Ja, Fritz voyna!*' What she was trying to say was that the Germans were hungry and defeated, with the inference that the brave Russian soldiers had conquered them.

The old man in the bed had been listening intently, subduing his anger and disgust, but he must have known this Russian word *voyna*. All at once his loathing got the better of him, for he thought Mother was saying that this was a 'German war', a 'Fritz war'. He sat upright in his bed and screamed, '*Nyet Fritz voyna! Zsid voyna! Jude voyna!*' ('Not a Fritz war! A Yid war! A Jewish war!') His face was twisted in rage; there were flecks of spittle on his lips.

We stared at him in amazement. To start with, we didn't know why he felt compelled to make this ludicrous claim, but moreover why he should risk his life by revealing his love of the Germans and his hatred of Jews at such a time. The Russians responded to the old man's outburst in quite a different way. Angered, they seized him, wrenched him from his bed and readied their rifles to shoot him.

Seeing what was about to happen, we rushed to intervene, and pleaded for the old man to be spared. He was a vile old man but still we did not want him shot. If the old man one day faced a higher judgement, well and good. But his blood should not be on our hands.

CHAPTER 20

Marienwerder

In the end, we accepted that we couldn't remain at the farmhouse. The Russian officer told us to take ourselves to a building that had been commandeered as the headquarters for the Red Army in the region – the 'Commandantura', as it was known. It was in a town some eight kilometres away. Once there, we would be required to register as refugees. The personnel at the Commandantura would consider our case and maybe find us lodgings. We were now no longer runaway Jews in danger of falling into the hands of the Nazis, but displaced persons likely to be considered simply nuisances alongside tens of thousands of other nuisances.

On the road to the Commandantura we passed Russian soldiers on their march towards Germany. They were a disorderly horde, and we quickly learned to dread them with almost as much intensity as we dreaded the SS. We knew we should be grateful to them for chasing the Germans out of our lives, but they looked like the cohorts of the Barbarian army on its way to sack Rome. The mixture of physical types was striking: slant-eyed Tartars, dark-skinned Armenians, Russians of the steppes with oddly upturned noses.

The Commandantura was located in a large family house, which was bursting at the seams with refugees, all with tales to tell the Russian officers. We overheard many people's stories as we waited our turn. The Russians had taken over the functions of the judiciary and the police, so they would intervene and restore order when necessary. The refugees told of rape, of theft, of Russian soldiers who had abandoned all discipline and given themselves over to their appetites. The officers were not much moved by the tales of rape and theft, but they were willing to register people as refugees.

When our turn came we were duly registered. It occurred to Mother to ask if there was any employment available, and it turned out there was. Mother and Erna were told to report to a cheese factory nearby. Marta was considered too weak to take on employment, and my bandaged arm and healing wound ruled me out.

Marta and I remained at the Commandantura while Mother and Erna took themselves off to the cheese factory. Their tasks were simple enough – washing huge rounds of hard cheese in an acidic solution that contributed to the ageing – but the hours were long and extended into the evening. The physical toll on both of them was great. All of us were suffering from boils on our bodies and from other aches and pains that had developed over months of inadequate nutrition, but it was particularly hard for my mother and sister, who stood on their aching legs for twelve-hour shifts. Other women and men, as wretched as us, also laboured away at the cheese factory.

We camped at the Commandantura overnight, and the next day Mother and Erna prepared for more toil. The stitches in my hand required attention, and Marta, who had never fully recovered from her fever and chilblains, also needed to be seen to by a doctor. Before she went off to work, Mother found a female Russian officer who gave us a sympathetic hearing. She directed us to a field hospital, where a doctor removed my stitches and dressed the wound again with a smaller bandage. Marta was examined, but whatever she was suffering from – probably typhus – couldn't be properly treated.

Afterwards we returned to the Commandantura to inform the female officer of our success in finding the field hospital. I don't know why we thought it necessary to do this, because the Commandantura was a dangerous place for us to be alone. There was a steady flow of Russian soldiers, all eager to find a girl with whom they could enjoy themselves. Marta and I were certainly noticed; we were referred to as 'the two pretty *vengerkas*' (the Russian word for Hungarian girls, as we learnt).

That day I grabbed Marta's hand and pulled her along as I searched for somewhere we could hide. In one empty room I found a big wooden wardrobe with doors that closed securely.

I stuffed Marta inside, forced myself in and pulled the doors shut. We listened in a state of near hysteria as the soldiers stomped about, searching for the *vengerkas*. The air inside the wardrobe stunk, and it was hot. Poor Marta was as weak as a kitten, and terrified.

After some hours huddled in the wardrobe, we heard a commotion: the gruff voices of soldiers, the cries of a young female. The distress of the girl made it apparent that she was being raped. I squeezed my eyes shut to intensify the darkness, as if this would hide me more completely. I prayed in silence for my mother to appear and somehow make the dread go away.

But we avoided the soldiers and survived the night. The next morning we met up again with Mother and Erna, who by now were convinced that Marta and I had disappeared. Our mother's relief when she saw us reduced her to tears.

The next day Mother went to see the Russian officer who was in charge of the cheese factory and said that the boils on her legs and Erna's made the time they spent standing at the trough washing cheeses a kind of torture. The officer was Jewish, and in fact bore a strong physical resemblance to my father. He allowed Mother to summarise (in Yiddish) the abuses she and her daughters had endured under the Nazis. He listened without any great sympathy. No doubt he had seen the death camps in his journey across Poland with his comrades, but he was unmoved. 'Madam, the war isn't over yet,' he said. 'We all have our duties.' For him the dogma of the Soviet state was stronger than the bond between Jews. And yet there was a happy outcome eventually: two weeks later my mother and Erna were transferred to a new workplace.

That new workplace was in the town of Kwidzyn, known in German as Marienwerder, back across the Vistula, one hundred kilometres south of Danzig. We travelled there by train. All of us were to be employed in a hospital in the vicinity of the town, where we would be stitching the military uniforms of shot Russian soldiers. Sewing machines were provided. We patched up the uniforms in the same way that surgeons patched up people; just as the surgeons sent the repaired people back to war, so we sent the repaired uniforms back to the soldiers.

Our lodgings at Marienwerder were a vast improvement on the Commandantura. We had an entire apartment in a big block, and we were the only tenants in the building. It was the last week of April 1945, and the spring sunshine streamed in through the windows of our first-floor flat, warming everything. Below us in the street, the Russian soldiers whom we had so feared a few days earlier were laughing and singing and playing tunes on harmonicas. One song in particular I adored, a Mexican folk song that had become famous all over the world. I began to hum the tune myself for the sheer pleasure of it.

In their celebrations, the soldiers wandered the streets of Marienwerder dressed comically in anything outrageous they could find in the empty dwellings of the town, even women's garments – shawls, silk dresses, women's hats. These soldiers had survived the war; their enemies, the Germans, were only a few days away from annihilation. Of course, some of the Russians were still perfectly capable of seizing women and girls and raping them, but in Marienwerder we could at least lock the door of our apartment against them. And the Russians here were less coarse, by and large, than those we'd encountered earlier. Most were gentlemen.

So for the first time we had a certain degree of comfort. What we ate was provided by the hospital: for breakfast sweet semolina cooked in fresh milk, served with freshly baked bread. And for dinner mince meat encased in pasta – a type of ravioli – smothered in delicious sauces. I can't say that I have ever relished food as much in my life as I did in Marienwerder.

From the room in which we worked at our sewing machines, we had a clear view into the brightly lit operating theatre of the hospital. The surgeons were kept busy day and night with casualties from the battlefield, even at this very late stage of the war. One of us would say, looking up from work, 'Dear God, now see what they're doing!' Usually they were amputating limbs too badly chewed up to be saved.

As seamstresses in Marienwerder, we were content to keep mending uniforms until we were repatriated home to Hungary. The only blight on our happy change of circumstances at this time came in the form of three Polish women, who were sent to live and work with us at the hospital. The eldest was about thirty, and ill-educated and coarse, and I could not feel any welcome in my heart for them. They said that they'd been working in Germany, that they'd become prisoners, and that the Russians had found them and sent them back to Poland.

The eldest of the three, Natasha, turned out to be an epileptic. One evening, as I was enjoying dinner with my mother and sisters at the kitchen table, Natasha came crashing through the door and fell to the floor, convulsing violently. We didn't think of epilepsy just at that moment; we thought Natasha had gone berserk, and we stood up ready to defend ourselves. Neither Natasha nor the other Polish girls had mentioned her epilepsy to us, so the episode frightened the daylights out of us. They didn't care what we thought – Natasha least of all.

Natasha regularly brought soldiers back to her bed at night – we all shared the one bedroom – and we were compelled to listen to the entertainment she provided for them. When my mother could stand it no longer, she upbraided Natasha. 'Is this the way to behave? Do you not see anything wrong in bringing your boyfriends here, where decent young women are sleeping? You are deplorable – tactless and tasteless.' Natasha merely shrugged, although she did find somewhere else to carry out her business.

It was in Marienwerder that I made a friend, Sasha. He was a Russian soldier who had until recently been a prisoner of the Germans, meaning that he would have suffered dreadfully. God knows how he survived, since the Germans murdered hundreds of thousands of their Russian prisoners. Sasha was a patient at the hospital, and he had noticed me when I came with one of the Polish girls to collect our food from the soldiers' mess hall there. He had made enquiries: 'That girl with the dark hair and the blue eyes – where does she live?' The Polish girl told him, and he came to visit me.

Sasha had a round, pleasant face, and he wore round glasses. He was quiet, educated, intelligent, well mannered and a little shy – everything that most Russian soldiers were not. 'Ochky Sasha', he came to be called – 'Sasha-with-the-specs'. He saw something in me that delighted him, I am happy to say – we were kindred spirits. He came often to the apartment to see me, and also Mother and Erna and Marta. We chatted with as much enjoyment as I could remember, mostly about books and poetry. I wouldn't say we were boyfriend and girlfriend, although that sort of attraction was certainly there. We didn't kiss – we didn't even touch – but we loved each other. We spoke sweetly to each other, and at every meeting he had something flattering to say about my looks, about my mind. Sasha was an honourable man who wished me to know that I would never find in him the sort of slobbering appetites that I had seen in his compatriots.

Sasha spoke competent German after his time in the POW camps, so with my bits and pieces of the language we were able to converse without strain. And he taught me Russian – how to speak it, read it and even write it. Even in the relatively short period of our friendship, Sasha's instruction gave me a good grasp of his native language.

The time came, inevitably, when Sasha was well enough to leave the hospital and rejoin his regiment. Having been a prisoner of war, he needed to redeem himself in the eyes of his fellow soldiers and officers, since it was considered a disgrace for a Russian soldier to be captured. Later, he wrote me lovely letters in Russian, at first in carefully composed Cyrillic print, then in longhand. I was able to read them without any great effort, and they thrilled and uplifted me. Whenever he wrote the phrase 'I love you', he put the words into Hungarian – *Szeretlek* – but in Cyrillic script. I still have the five letters he sent me.

My mother and my sisters also picked up enough Russian to allow us to converse with the soldiers, and that made everything easier. In fact, our lives were altogether so much easier than at any time over the past year. We even managed to add a few items to our household by wandering around Marienwerder and inspecting the interiors of the many empty houses in the town. We didn't consider that we were looting. These empty places had been abandoned by ethnic Germans fleeing the Russians, and would very likely remain abandoned. Some of the orphaned items we adopted were merely practical – kitchen utensils and the like – but some were lovely, such as an exquisite pearl embroidery which is now framed and displayed in my home. My mother kept for many years a small blue crystal vase she found in a Marienwerder house.

One day, with no warning at all, we were told to pack up and go to the station, where we would board a train to the city of Stettin, three hundred kilometres west of Marienwerder. (Stettin was then part of Germany, but a few months later became Polish territory and was renamed Szczecin.) At the station we realised that the entire staff of the hospital was boarding the train.

It was a long journey, and the mood amongst the passengers, especially the Russian soldiers, was cheerful and relaxed. There was a great deal of singing accompanied by the harmonica, and smiling Russian faces all around us. We were special favourites of the soldiers, this time in a good way – they weren't about to assault us.

The scene we saw through the windows as we travelled west was one of devastation. Germany had been bombed to smithereens. Many towns and villages were reduced to rubble. People stood like wraiths amidst the ruins, their faces haggard. When the Jewish women of Auschwitz were sent by train to Stutthof, I had seen well-dressed, well-fed Polish and ethnic German civilians, and I had both envied and resented them. How things had changed. In the eight months since then, millions of tonnes of bombs had been dropped from the sky on this region. Now I pitied the people we saw.

There was a question we asked all those we met, or at least those who we thought might have the answer: 'Have you met anyone who came from a concentration camp?' We were always told, 'No, not a soul.' Apart from the Red Army officer who supervised the cheese factory, we had not come across another Jew. We came to think that we were the only Jews left. But we held out hope that some would emerge from hiding when peace came. Of course, the one we most wished to embrace was our father.

The train stopped one evening some way from Stettin. A soldier made enquiries, then told us that the rails ahead were damaged and would be repaired overnight. We alighted from the carriage and shuffled down an embankment to open fields. There was no station and no town to be seen. Soldiers were busily erecting their tents in the fading light. Those of us who were not soldiers were given large squares of carpet from which to fashion shelters, and a couple of blankets each. We didn't attempt to build a proper hut but simply constructed a type of shelter, with a carpet square on the ground and blankets slung between four stakes as walls, but open to the sky. The night was mild, with no prospect of rain. We settled on our backs and gazed up at the heavens, where a million stars glittered. I found myself smiling at them, blessing their beauty. I was still smiling when I fell asleep.

An hour or two later I was awoken by the sound of gunfire. I raised myself and saw the faces of my mother and my sisters in the moonlight, their expressions as alarmed as my own. The gunfire intensified and the four of us began whimpering in despair. Tracers of many colours criss-crossed the night sky. The Russians had abandoned us in our sleep! The Germans had come back and we would be captured a second time! I was not so much breathing as panting, in short, shallow gasps. To come so close to safety only to become captives once more was a horrific prospect.

'What is happening?' I whispered to my mother.

We clung to each other, Mother, Erna, Marta and me. At that moment, if we'd had the power to choose oblivion, I think we would have done so. The knot of pain in my heart was the worst I'd ever known.

Then someone lifted the blanket wall and looked in. 'Girls, girls, wake up!' a voice shouted. 'The war has ended! The war has ended!' It was a Russian soldier, smiling with glistening teeth. 'Wake up, girls! Come and celebrate! The war is finished! *Voyna zakonchilas!*'

CHAPTER 21

Return

We did not know that the German city of Stettin would become the Polish city of Szczecin within the year. Nor did we know that our native Hungary would bend to the will and rule of the Russians. We knew nothing at all of the way in which Europe was to be carved up.

It was the middle of May 1945. Mother, with her gift for home-making, turned our barren new apartment into a warm and welcoming place. We were beginning to resemble proper human beings once more – quite well dressed for the season. In the ghost town of Stettin, the only other people on the streets were Russian soldiers. Most of the other women were Russian nurses and military personnel, many of them pretty but not fashionable.

One lovely Sunday afternoon, Erna and I decided to attend a big regional concert being staged by the Russians. When we were on the train coming to Stettin, one of the soldiers had serenaded us on his harmonica with Brahms' 'Hungarian Rhapsody'. The soldiers had suggested that we Hungarian girls might like to dance with them to the Brahms rhapsody in the future.

The concert was being staged in an enormous hall. By the time we arrived, dressed in white blouses and plain skirts, it was already packed with soldiers and nurses. We stood at the back, a long way from the podium. A couple of smart young soldiers approached us, made gentlemanly bows and asked us to follow them. Erna and I winked at each other to show we were game, and we allowed ourselves to be escorted all the way to the front row, where a fat Red Army general was seated. We were ushered to seats on either side of the general, who was by no means a young or good-looking man. He had rows of medals and ribbons on the breast of his uniform jacket, and when he smiled at Erna and me he displayed a mouth full of gold teeth. I thought: 'Dear God, what have we got ourselves into?'

Still, we sat cheerfully through the concert, applauded all the acts and tried to look moved when the Russians on stage sang sentimental ballads. At the conclusion of each item on the program, the general would ask us questions about our lives back in Hungary and pay us compliments on our beauty. We, in turn, asked him about life in Russia, and complimented him on his great success against the *Wehrmacht*.

After the final item, the general turned to Erna and invited the two of us to join him afterwards. 'Big party,' he said. 'Food, drink. We all laugh and sing! You come to the big party.'

'Comrade General,' Erna replied, 'we must apologise and decline; our mother will be expecting us home.'

The general was appalled. We were refusing a party with the glorious, victorious Russian soldiers?

'Many apologies, Comrade General, but our mother worries about us like crazy,' Erna said. 'We must get home.'

The general was offended, and left in a huff.

For us, Stettin was a relief. Through June, July and August we were well-fed and relaxed. Nothing much was happening. The Russians went about their work, whatever it was; a few of the locals who'd left the city before the Russian occupation drifted back. After a period of rest, we were sent to work in the kitchens that prepared food for the Russian military. It wasn't hard work, and it gave us access to all the food we could possibly eat.

There were no complaints from me, or from Erna or Marta, but something was stirring in our mother. Her birthday came around on the twenty-ninth of August. Back in Nyírbátor, we had always made a big fuss of her, but all we could do in Stettin was sit by her bedside and wish her a happy birthday.

'Girls, I have something to say,' she began. 'I couldn't sleep all night. I was terribly sad. I was remembering past birthdays, all of them, in Nyírbátor. Suddenly I realised who I am, who we are. I said to myself, "Boeske, enough is enough – it is time to take your daughters home." Girls, we are going back to Nyírbátor.'

None of us had spoken much before about 'going home'. It was as if the whole idea of a return to Nyírbátor had become unthinkable. My mother's imagination was the first to awaken. My reaction to the prospect of another upheaval, though, was delight. I was very moved by Mother's profound conviction.

All over Germany, millions of people were on the move. The Germans themselves were desperate for shelter, and for employment, and they would go anywhere just to find a tiny bit of comfort. Millions of others – non-Germans, former captives – were also struggling to reach their homelands. We knew that train travel was the only possibility, but we also knew that the railways of Germany, bombed to pieces, only carried a few trains at this time. Those trains that did run – and we had seen some passing through Stettin – were packed with passengers; people would hang from the sides of the carriages, or even climb onto the roofs. Only the Russian soldiers travelled inside the train. They had the authority to order all other passengers out.

'Do we not belong to the Red Army?' my mother said. 'Have we not worked for the Russians for months? I will ask them to give us a special pass, one that says we are special friends of the Red Army and can travel in the carriages.'

As we served meals to the Russian big shots, we were able to make a special request of them. But they were annoyed that we weren't going with them to Russia. Few people, however, were as persistent as my mother, and gradually she wore down the officer in command of the Stettin forces. 'Please,' she pleaded. 'We have served the glorious army of the Soviet Union but now it is time for us to return to our home. So please give us a pass that will allow us to travel in the train carriages with the Russian soldiers.'

It took ten days but my mother prevailed. A soldier brought us a sheet of paper on which something in Russian was scrawled. The words said that we were authorised to travel in train carriages all over Germany. And there was a less official note at the end: 'But go now to your home, ungrateful people, if you don't want to come with us to Russia.' We gathered up our few possessions, our bedding and clothing, and hurried down to the railway station as fast as our legs could carry us.

And so we commenced our journey back to Hungary. Our travel certificate was at times accepted, at times not. On good days we found a place for ourselves in carriages; on bad days we packed ourselves on as best we could. Every carriage was stuffed full of humanity, many struggling like us to find our lives again. We stopped here and there. At one station Erna and I went in search of food, and approached the station master to ask for directions. We knew instantly that we'd chosen the wrong man. Lust bloomed on his face and without the least hesitation he began to grope us. We escaped him.

Finally we were in a carriage taking us to Berlin. A woman on the train, a German woman but certainly not a Nazi, told my mother of a place in Berlin that catered to displaced Jews. 'I have the address for you,' she said, and wrote it on a slip of paper. 'The people there will help you, I am sure.'

We came at last to Lehrter Bahnhof in Berlin. It had been badly damaged by bombs, but a few platforms were functioning, the rubble cleared away. It was a pleasant autumn afternoon. Mother approached people in the streets and asked directions to the address of the organisation that assisted Jews. And we found it: an intact building amongst thousands that had been destroyed. A garden thrived at the front of the building, and a path led us to an impressive entrance. We sat at a garden table and waited.

A woman in a nurse's uniform appeared. Speaking German, she called out to us: 'Happy new year!' We looked at each other, puzzled. What was she talking about? It was September. Then understanding dawned on us: it was the eve of Rosh Hashanah, the Jewish new year. The significance of this moved each of us – my mother, Erna, Marta and me.

The relief organisation headquarters was a place where Jews could catch their breath, as it were, and consider their options. We decided we would stay in Berlin for ten days, until the day after Yom Kippur, when we would take a train to Hungary. We met others who also wished to return to their former homes, and who hoped to find that their relatives and friends had done the same. There were also those who did not expect to meet their children, husbands, wives, sisters, brothers, sweethearts, aunts, uncles or cousins ever again. Some knew about the deaths of their dear ones. Many of these Jews would choose to migrate to countries outside Europe – America, Canada or Australia – for who could ever again trust Europe? Some would choose Palestine, where the state of Israel was being promoted as a homeland for the Jews.

Jewish agencies that promoted resettlement in Palestine were active in Europe at that time. 'Israel is coming,' they said. 'Live with us in Israel. Never again will you be marched from your houses at gunpoint.' In the synagogue attached to the relief organisation's building, Jews with broken lives gathered to tell their stories. Sometimes we prayed; sometimes we sat without uttering a word.

In the synagogue, stories were told all day long. '*We were taken to Bergen-Belsen in the north ... We went to Monowitz, a terrible place ... to Majdanek ... to Chełmno ...*' Not all the stories were of suffering, though. Many spoke of everyday matters – of where they had found lodgings, of their plans for the future, even of new romances. But the two great themes of the stories we heard in the synagogue were 'I have suffered' and 'This I will now do'. For me, it was arresting to see the often calm and deliberate expressions of people as they spoke about taking up their lives where they had left off years earlier.

At the synagogue we came to know a nice young man from Poland named Aron. At the relief organisation headquarters he had met and fallen in love with a Hungarian girl called Eva, who had since departed Berlin for Hungary. He spoke of her with tenderness and longing. When we revealed to this lovelorn fellow that we too were Hungarians, he began to bubble with excitement. He wanted to help us in any way he could, as if by coming to our aid he would be honouring his love for his absent sweetheart. He even offered to pay for our train fares to Hungary. 'Ladies, I'll come with you on the train to Budapest,' he said.

'And you can help me find Eva.' We quickly agreed.

From Berlin to Budapest is a journey of more than a day, but we had seats in a carriage with our young friend and it wasn't such an ordeal. Aron chattered incessantly about his girlfriend the whole way. We only half listened, distracted by the emotions filling our hearts as we returned home sixteen months after being forced from it. Seeing road signs and station names in Hungarian moved me to tears.

At the Budapest-Nyugati railway station we saw a familiar face: Vera Feleki, the elder sister of my first childhood sweetheart, Gyuri. Vera, it turned out, was not alone in the world. She and her lover ran a hotel in Budapest, and she insisted that we come and stay there. We were standing together just outside the station in Budapest, which hadn't been badly bombed.

There was a question we had to ask Vera, although we dreaded the answer. But my mother asked.

'Your husband did not return, Boeske,' Vera said. 'And, Baba, Gyuri did not return either.'

More than six months had passed since the liberation of the camps, and anyone found alive had been documented. If my father had survived, it would be known by now. It came as no great shock to have it confirmed that he'd perished, and yet at the same time it did. But we did not weep – not there and then.

Vera also told us that the rounding up of Jews in Budapest had not been as thorough as in the regional towns and cities. Some had remained hidden, or had been able to bribe officials to overlook them. Churches had become sanctuaries for a significant number. Others had obtained documentation that permitted them to pass as Christians. Foreign embassies had taken in thousands of Jews, Vera said. One way or another, a certain number of Jews had eluded the Hungarians and the SS. Those who had not – some hundreds of thousands – had been forced to march without food or shelter towards Germany. It was said that tens of thousands of Jews had died on these marches.

This news gave us hope that our Budapest relatives, the Lichtmans, might still be alive in the city. They were my mother's sister's family. We had no reason to believe that they would be amongst the Budapest Jews who had survived, but we wanted to believe it.

We went with Vera to her hotel and were shown to a room, and then we hurried to the Lichtmans' address, 1 Jókai Tér, in a suburb of the city. As we rode the tram, I thought of how my aunt Marta and her family had made me so welcome on my only visit to Budapest years ago. We held out hope that Aunt Marta, her husband, Armin, and my cousins were still alive.

But it was too much to hope for. We reached the Lichtmans' house, only to find it occupied by another family. The man who answered our knock on the door had never heard of them. He only knew that the family who had lived there before him were long gone – to where, he had no idea.

We returned crestfallen to Vera's hotel and told her of our disappointment. But then we learned from her that other relatives of ours had definitely survived: Boeske's half-brother, Feivi

The Lichtman family before the war, about 1937.
From left: Moshe, aged about nine, Marta (Boeske's only full sister), Kati and Armin.
Moshe survived and went to Israel. Marta and Armin were taken away and didn't
return. Kati, the young photographer who took the photo of Baba on page 84, ended
up in a ghetto in Bratislava and starved herself to death.
In the early 1940s many young Jewish men of Budapest were arrested and held in a
town called Kistarcsa. Armin dedicated himself completely to staying in touch with
those men and assisting them in any way he could.

Gutman, his wife, Bolyika, and their children, Gitta and Yankele, were living in Debrecen. The news lifted our spirits, but I stifled my delight; I didn't want another disappointment.

We left Budapest between Yom Kippur and Sukkot, having found a place for ourselves on the train to Debrecen. There, we found the Gutmans alive and thriving. It was like swallowing some fabulous tonic that revives you within seconds. We kissed, we hugged, we wept.

The Gutmans' story was absorbing. They had all been sent to a camp in Austria, and they would surely have been murdered had not Eichmann, the Nazi minister in charge of the murder of Jews, chosen them as one of the Jewish families at Theresienstadt to be spared. In 1944, when it became apparent to many in the SS that Germany would be defeated, a deal was made to save some Jewish families, who would be exhibited to the invading Allies as examples of the compassionate treatment of Jews. The scheme was an utter fraud, of course, but it allowed the Gutmans to survive. They were kept in Austria, fed and sheltered, until the very end of the war. Thus, the Gutmans were amongst the small proportion of European Jewish families – of those who remained in Europe – still intact in May 1945.

At Debrecen we fulfilled our obligations to recall the dead in a ritual way. We remembered my grandfather, Ignac Yitzchak Kellner, who was seventy-four when he was taken from the train carriage at Auschwitz and expired there beside the rails. And of course we remembered my father, Gyula Yechiel Keimovits, who gave us life and his name. He was a man so beloved, so tender and supportive that even today, when I am at an age much greater than he ever reached, I recall him with tears and pain.

We also remembered Aunt Klara and my cousins Mira, Mimi and Katika. I told the Gutmans about the day Mira was taken. 'She was holding my hand,' I said. 'There was such chaos – we didn't know that one line was for the gas chamber, and the other for the sheds of the living. But even if she'd known, Mira would have gone with her mother and sisters.'

We did not yet know about the other Kellner relatives who had perished. Shloime Kellner, his wife, Basha, and three of their four children were dead: Shloime in a labour camp, Basha and the three children in the gas chamber. Their eldest son, Yossi, survived, and in time went to live in Israel. He and many other prisoners were abandoned by the SS in a railway carriage at the end of the war. They spent twelve days in freezing weather, finally being released by the soldiers of the advancing Red Army. Yossi was amongst the few still alive when the carriage door was flung open. Manci Moshkovits, my mother's youngest half-sister, and her husband, Moishe, were both killed. And of course there were the Lichtmans, whom we'd hurried to embrace in Budapest. Seventeen of my mother's immediate family, all killed.

We took the train to Nyírbátor and walked from the railway station into the town. Everything we saw was familiar, and yet it wasn't. The streets, the acacia trees, the houses, the shops – everything was transformed by what we had experienced. We were not the people who had been taken from the town on carts eighteen months earlier.

I recalled that, as we left Nyírbátor all that time ago, I had sworn to have my revenge. Now I had returned, and my revenge was that I was still alive. My life would go on.

CHAPTER 22

Home

We were home, but we were also homeless. We had lived in a number of rented houses in Nyírbátor after my parents sold the house at 1 Pócsi Utca, so there was nowhere for us to return to. But by enquiring here and there, we came to realise that we were not the first Jews to have come back to the town. In fact we were almost the last: all the other surviving Jews of Nyírbátor – one hundred and thirty out of three thousand – had found their way back.

Amongst them was my father's cousin, Yakab Kramer, together with his son Mishi – the boy who gave us the news of the German occupation of Budapest. 'We did not know that we would ever see you again,' Yakab said. 'And now you will stay with us until you find a way ahead.'

We stayed with Yakab and Mishi for a week or so, then we moved into Grandfather Kellner's old house, living in the half that had been occupied by Lipe and Klara's family. Once more

The Russian army commemorated the first anniversary of the liberation of Hungary in Nyírbátor on 5 April 1946. Baba and Marta, by now Russian speakers, took part in the event.

we told our stories, this time to Yakab and Mishi and other Jews we met in the town. My stomach became painfully knotted whenever I spoke about our experiences.

Just across the street was the synagogue, and much of the furniture that had once belonged to the Jews of Nyírbátor had been stored there since April 1944, the time of our expulsion. We picked our way through what was left, which was not much, as those who had returned to Nyírbátor earlier than us had taken most of it. We found nothing of ours.

Not long afterwards, my mother was visiting a neighbour and noticed that the dining table and the chairs bore a startling resemblance to our own table and bentwood chairs. She made a claim on them, startling the woman, who'd found them in the synagogue. 'Well, people can say that anything belongs to them,' the woman said. 'Where's your proof?'

My mother told the woman that if she turned all the chairs upside down, she would find the following sentence written on the bottom of one: 'If I cannot marry the Prince of Wales, I will marry no one.' I had written this when I was thirteen; the Prince of Wales was courting Wallis Simpson at the time, and it was all over the news. They upended the chairs and found the proof. My mother reclaimed her table and chairs, and they were carried back to our own kitchen – much to the chagrin of the woman who had enjoyed ownership of them for a few months.

Of course, we had buried our big wooden crate in the back garden of our landlords' place in April 1944. My mother's younger unmarried brother, Bimi, who had survived in Budapest under the Germans, had already dug it up for us. He had emerged from hiding in January 1945 and decided to go to Nyírbátor to live. Once there, he had paid a visit to our old landladies, to enquire if we had left anything with them. They told him of the crate buried in the back garden. The rain that season was steady and persistent, and the old ladies were worried that whatever was in the crate would spoil. Bimi dug it up, and sure enough, most of what was inside had been ruined by water seeping in. He took what he could to Grandfather's house: some of Erna's trousseau; the silver candlestick holder; the water-damaged photo albums; the demijohn of goose fat. They were symbolic of our lives after the Shoah: damaged, and in certain respects unable to be repaired.

Soon after moving into Aunt Klara's house, we opened a shop – the same shop that Erna and Mother had managed before we were taken away. As it happened, Klara's husband, Lipe, had run a haberdasher's shop. When the Jews of the town were being rounded up, he took the goods from the shop and stored them in the shaft of a skylight. The festival of Sukkot was coming and we decided to build a *sukka* by opening that skylight and setting up palm fronds as its roof, as the Jewish law prescribes. We opened the panel that sealed off the skylight, and down tumbled the socks, handkerchiefs, gloves, and odds and ends of Lipe's shop. We saw in this raining down of gloves and socks from above a sign that our plan to revive our shop accorded with God's wishes. We stocked our shop and opened for business.

One day a young man named Andor Schwartz came into the shop. He had heard that I wanted to buy a few US dollars, and he needed some Hungarian forints to buy groceries. Andor had lived in Budapest for much of the war, even though many of his family had stayed in Nyírbátor. After the Germans invaded on the nineteenth of March, 1944, he was conscripted into the Labour Service in Kassa. He soon escaped and went to Budapest. He survived on his wits for some months, and then found refuge in the Swiss embassy until liberation by the Red Army on the nineteenth of January, 1945. Andor made his way back to Nyírbátor alone.

He went to his family home, and found it empty. He came to know from various sources that all those dear to him had died in the slaughter. On the floor of the house was what Andor recognised at a glance as his family tree; it had formerly been framed and displayed on the wall. The watercolour painting of a tree – with trunk, branches and foliage – showed the generations of his family going back to the 1700s. He felt as if he were being mocked in his grief.

Andor's suffering was such that he lay down on the floor of that house, with no wish to move again. His father, mother, brother, sister and cousins had all vanished from the face of the earth, and he alone was left. He lay in a lifeless state for three days, and he repudiated God.

After those three days Andor's friends heard of his despair and came to the house. 'Andor Schwartz, what is this?' they asked.

'You must rouse yourself and face life.' He didn't move. 'Many have suffered,' his friends said. 'You are not the only one. Rouse yourself, find your courage.' Still Andor did not move. His friends knelt around him and repeated their entreaties, and finally he climbed to his feet.

'I will find courage,' he said. 'But this is my vow: I will keep a kosher household, I will lay tefillin, but I will never again say Hallel. I will not sing the praise of the God who allowed my family to be taken from me.'

All this took place before we returned to Nyírbátor; Andor later told me the story. In fact I had met him before we were expelled and taken to Auschwitz. I had invited him to a party; I'd wanted to introduce him to a girlfriend of mine with the idea that he would take to her. But he didn't come – he went back to Budapest instead. Of course, Andor, if he'd wished, could have had the pick of all the girls. He was more than handsome. He was also intelligent and had a charisma that drew people to him. Still, I wasn't crazy about him. I needed to mature before I could appreciate what was in Andor.

It was December 1945, late in the month, when I saw Andor again. By this time he was twenty-one, and was making one of his regular visits to Nyírbátor. I invited him to the Saint Sylvester party my mother was organising. The feast of Saint Sylvester falls on the thirty-first of December, New Year's Eve, and everyone celebrates. This time I was hoping to fix him up with my friend Zsuzsi. Andor and I chatted for a while but I had no designs on him myself. In any case, Andor said he wouldn't be attending the party.

'That's okay,' I said. 'You don't have to go if you don't wish to.'

'If you're not there, there will be no celebration,' he replied.

That was the first indication of his interest in me. I had always thought he was more interested in Marta.

We had scarcely opened our shop when Erna married Sanyi Grosz and declared her intention of travelling to a Displaced Persons camp in Germany to register as a prospective immigrant to Australia, or to Canada, if not America. She did not trust Europe; she did not believe that this was the last of all Holocausts. And so we farewelled them on the train. Soon after that we closed the shop.

There was nothing for us girls to do in Nyírbátor. Mother was concerned for us and decided to send us to a Zionist girls' home in Budapest. I instantly became an ardent Zionist, so much so that my mother called me an extremist. The look of conviction on my face must have startled the less committed. After about a month there Marta and I came home to Nyírbátor, and I announced loudly: 'I'm going to Israel!'

'All right, sure,' my mother said. 'But what about me?'

'Oh, I hadn't thought about that,' I said, feeling selfish.

Around this time Mother's sister-in-law had proposed a match for her, but she hadn't taken it seriously until that moment. Her daughters would be starting lives of their own, and she had to find a new life for herself too. The man she'd been matched with went by the name of Laci Schneck. Both were in their

The celebration of Bela (Bill) Gross's brit milah in a Displaced Persons' camp in Ansbach, Germany, on 13 October 1947.
Erna is at the left end of the bottom row, and her husband, Sanyi Grosz, is second from the right in the middle row (next to the man reading a prayer book).

middle forties, which made it one of the few matches at the time between two mature Jews. Most European Jewish women in their thirties were dead, sent to the gas chambers with their young children in the camps. Almost all those who survived were young women, like me and my sisters. My mother survived only because she looked younger than she actually was.

Mother went off to Debrecen to meet Schneck while Marta and I were still in Nyírbátor, intending to return to the girls' home in Budapest. Marta did not approve of my mother remarrying with what seemed like haste, but I had no objection. There were very few men of her age to choose from. Those who had survived the Shoah were mostly marrying girls half their age. So Mother and Schneck were engaged, and Schneck went to Debrecen to spend Rosh Hashanah and Yom Kippur with the Gutman family. Mother stayed there too.

I had been sure that she wouldn't leave her daughters to celebrate the high holidays by ourselves, but I was wrong. In a strange way, though, it was a good thing that she left us alone for a while. At this time Marta and I gave full vent to our mourning. At the synagogue I sat at my mother's seat with her bronze nameplate and cried like I had never cried before. I talked to my father, telling him about everything that had happened since his death. I told him that Boeske was no longer his wife: she would soon be Mrs Schneck.

Marta and I returned to the girls' camp in Budapest. Across the Danube there was another camp, where young Zionists were trained for agriculture in Israel. It was known as the *hachshara*,

Boeske in 1945, before she married Schneck.

the Hebrew word for preparation. Marta and I spent a few enjoyable months there. We learnt Hebrew, we danced, we sang and were among comrades, all intent on *aliyah*.

My mother, meanwhile, contacted me and Marta to say that she had accepted Schneck's proposal of marriage. She asked me to go to Nyírbátor and pack up the house. Our time at the girls' home was at an end in any case, and my determination to go to Israel was undiminished. Marta and I would stay with my Uncle Bimi in Budapest to get ready to leave for Israel.

Andor visited me while I was packing up the house. He wore a smart shirt, a sleeveless jumper, slacks, a fur-lined leather jacket, and boots that laced up in a complicated way – everything he ever wore complemented his good looks. He wanted me to marry him, he said.

In Budapest, I knew, he was the darling of numerous ladies, any one of whom would have walked over broken glass to hear him say, 'Will you marry me?' So I treated his proposal as a joke. 'Marry me?' I said. 'Really? I'm not what you're looking for. I'm irresponsible, I'm lazy, I would never get the housework done.' I recognised that we were perfect for each other, but at the same time perfectly wrong.

At the end of our conversation, Andor went back to Budapest, probably relieved that I'd declined his offer of marriage. I was just as relieved that I'd wriggled out of becoming Mrs Schwartz.

When I went to stay with Uncle Bimi in Budapest, I wrote a letter to Andor on a typewriter in the study. I composed it as an anonymous letter, as if from some well-wisher who had only his

Baba is fourth from the left, standing. Marta is directly below her, and their cousin Yossi Kellner is the man without a shirt at the extreme right. He did migrate to Israel, and lived on a kibbutz. The goose at the front is a joke, referring to the logo of the humorous magazine Lúdas Matyi.

best interests at heart, and I explained why he should never think of marrying Baba Keimovits. It was as if I might embrace Andor's marriage proposal against my will, and so I was making a pre-emptive renunciation. Also, I didn't yet wish to give up my liberty as a single woman. I had my plans to go to Israel, as I had told Andor. He was not attracted to the idea of sailing off to Haifa. I folded the typewritten letter, slipped it into an envelope and posted it to Andor.

My anonymous letter was written and posted at a time of confusion in Hungary. The war had been over for almost eighteen months, and it was widely accepted that the Russians would make all the important decisions in the country, now and in the future. But private enterprise was still permitted. Andor was a clever man with a head for business, and I thought of him as thriving and prosperous. As a matter of fact, Andor was broke. He had made a load of money in tobacco on the black market, and had confidently bought truckloads of cigarettes, storing them in a warehouse. With no warning, the government appointed by the Russians declared a state monopoly on tobacco, and Andor's warehouse of cigarettes was rendered worthless.

I knew nothing of this, and thought of him as a wealthy young man. Not that it mattered, because I wasn't going to marry him. Or maybe I would marry him. Actually, I doubted it. Then I was certain again …

I had yet to see my mother since her marriage to Schneck, and so I decided to arrange to make a visit to Banhegyes, where they were living. When I called her on the phone, I told her that

The hachshara, or preparation camp to migrate to Palestine, in Rona Utca, Pest. Top: Baba dances with other young people. She is at the top centre, framed by entryway to the building behind.

I was engaged – even though I was far from sure that I was. Mother let out a shriek. 'Dear God! What are you telling me?' Before I told her the name of the man to whom I was engaged, I reminded her that she had already given her approval. 'What? Baba, are you mad? I gave no approval!'

'Yes, Mother. Once, when Andor came to visit us with a friend, you said: "He would make a good husband for one of my girls."'

'Nonsense! I said no such thing.'

'Mother, it's Andor Schwartz.'

'Andor Schwartz? You are engaged to Andor Schwartz?'

'Yes, I am.'

Was I? Yes. No. Maybe.

My head in a muddle, I took the train to Banhegyes on a Friday. It was a slow train, and I realised in the middle of the journey that I would not reach my destination before Shabbat. I would have to break my journey at Békéscsaba and spend a day with a friend in the town, Ibi. I went through all the reasons why I should and should not marry Andor with her, and by the time I reached Banhegyes, I had decided that I would become his wife. I was greeted by my mother and her new husband. After hugs and kisses, I asked if I could use the telephone. I dialled Andor's number. 'I accept your proposal,' I said. 'We'll get married.' I would become Mrs Schwartz.

Andor and Baba at the time of their engagement, 1946.

CHAPTER 23

Hallel

On my return to Budapest, I met Andor at Uncle Bimi's house. But instead of gaiety and hurrahs and jubilation, he led me to the typewriter in the study – he knew where to find it. He said, 'Baba, sit down and type me something.' He had my anonymous letter in his hand, and he wanted to see if the type matched. Reluctantly, I typed a few lines and Andor compared what I'd written with the letter. I conceded that what Andor suspected was true, but he didn't make me suffer over it.

Our wedding was at the Gutmans' house in Debrecen on the twenty-sixth of January, 1947. It was a freezing cold day, with snowstorms and howling winds. My mother was to come with Schneck in his truck, but when it was time to go under the *chuppah*, she hadn't arrived. We waited and waited, but there was no sign of them. I sat there, on the *kallah*'s festive seat, and wept with worry. Finally they arrived, and we stood under the *chuppah*, shivering, Andor in his fur coat and long boots, and me in a hired short fur and with eyes red from crying. The day ended joyfully, though, with dancing and singing.

We started married life in Andor's house in Nyírbátor. I hadn't been there before, and as I entered I saw an enormous carved bookshelf, stacked with all the classics: English, French and Russian authors, all translated into Hungarian. I was delighted: I had made a good marriage after all!

After the debacle of the cigarettes, Andor entered into an arrangement with two partners to run a flour mill, but it didn't work out. He heard of another mill, this one in Vámospércs, some fifty kilometres east of Debrecen. The family who owned it weren't really interested in selling but needed capital to renew the machinery. Andor borrowed ten thousand forints from my Uncle Bimi and negotiated a fifty per cent partnership. The mill prospered and we were able to live a good life. We repaid Uncle Bimi in next to no time.

Within a few months I was pregnant. I insisted that the baby would be delivered at home. 'It was good enough for my grandmother, good enough for my mother, and it's good enough for me,' I said. And I knew my mother would be there at my bedside.

The baby was born at two o'clock on the morning of the eleventh of March, 1948. It was a healthy boy, and after his first bath they brought him to me. His big blue eyes seemed to take in everything with great curiosity. Andor, the man who had lost his whole family in the Shoah, held his son. We named him Moshe, after Andor's beloved father.

Exhausted, everyone went to sleep. We awoke on Rosh Chodesh Adar Sheni, the first day of Adar, the day of the new moon. It is said that the arrival of Adar brings joy, and for us it did. This is a day on which Hallel is always recited. But not by Andor, of course.

I was lying with my baby in the bedroom. Andor had arranged a *minyan*, a quorum of men, to pray and to celebrate. He came into the bedroom and said, 'Give me the child.' He took the baby to the next room, where the men were gathered. He introduced the boy to the congregation. 'Here is my son! His name is Moshe Schwartz.'

And then I heard a booming voice, unmistakeably Andor's. He was intoning loudly to make sure I heard him from the next room. My heart was filled with joy. He was reciting the Hallel.

The Schwartz house in Moshav Shafir, Israel.

Afterword

by Morry Schwartz

Israel   By April 1949 Hungary was moving towards Communism. Sensing a new threat, the Schwartz family decided to leave their new life and business behind.

On the thirteenth of May, 1949, with the aid of people smugglers, Baba, Andor – with the fourteen-month-old Moshe on his back – and Andor's cousin Joli walked under cover of night through a Carpathian forest to the Czechoslovakian border.

They reached Košice, then travelled by train to Vienna, where they spent time in a Displaced Persons camp. Deciding to migrate to Israel, they took a train to Bari in Italy, then boarded a rusty old battleship, the *Atzmaut*. Three days later, on the fast day of Tisha B'Av (the fourth of August, 1949), they arrived in the port city of Haifa.

They settled in a newly established agricultural village, Moshav Shafir, near Migdal Ashkelon. All the inhabitants were young refugee families from Hungary. It was a difficult pioneering life, lived at first in tents. They built houses and worked the land and created new lives for themselves.

On the twenty-eighth of August, 1952, Baba and Andor's second son, Eli (Alan), was born.

Life became easier over time. For a while Andor served in the army. Baba began teaching herself English, for by 1958 they had decided to leave Israel. Andor was ambitious and longed for a life in the West; for her part, Baba was keen to reunite with her sisters, who were already living in Australia.

Baba, Moshe (Morry) and Andor in Shafir, circa 1950.

Joli, Moshe (Morry), Baba and baby Eli (Alan), 1952.

Andor, Eli (Alan) and Baba ploughing a field.

Enjoying entertainment in Shafir. Andor sits on the far left; Yehuda Rabin is next to him. Fourth from the left is Yossi Mondshein, and Moshe is to his left.

Marta (left) with Atara Gutman, Baba's beloved cousin, in Tel Aviv, circa 1952.

Baba in front of the Kadima theatre, Tel Aviv, 1952.

The Schwartz family on a stopover in Manila on the way to Australia.

Australia   In 1949 Boeske and her second husband, Laci Schneck, had migrated to New York. A few months earlier Erna, Sanyi and baby Bill had travelled to live in Melbourne, and a year or so later Marta and Ernest joined them.

Even though Andor and Baba had very little money, Andor decided the family would travel to Australia in style. In September 1958 they boarded an Air France propeller plane, and four days later – having stopped over in Manila – they arrived at Essendon Airport.

At first life in Melbourne was dispiriting and difficult. Andor worked as a labourer, including time at General Motors Holden, while Baba taught Hebrew and was an overlocker in a shirt factory.

Six months after their arrival they borrowed money and bought a dairy farm in Nar Nar Goon, Gippsland. Andor's farming instincts returned and they spent two happy years there, becoming Australians. The easy kindness of their neighbours after a fire in the kitchen of their little fibro farmhouse was a heartwarming welcome to their new country.

In 1962 they sold the farm at a good profit, but unwisely bought a café, the Manhattan, in Dandenong, where they lost what they had made. With what was left they bought a milk bar in Richmond, but walked away from it within weeks.

Laid low but undaunted, Andor again borrowed money and bought a boarding house. This was to be the beginning of his career as a successful developer of property.

The family's third son, Danny, was born on the sixteenth of August, 1962. Soon after, they moved to 74 Balaclava Road, Caulfield, which was to become their long-term family home.

Baba worked alongside Andor as he built a successful business, but she used all her spare time to read and study. She graduated with a degree in English Literature from Monash University, and she taught herself Italian.

Andor published his memoir, *Living Memory*, in 2003, when he was seventy-nine. He passed away at the age of ninety on the twelfth of April, 2014.

Baba moved into an apartment in the city hotel that Andor built. There, she thrills at the views of the Yarra River, the bay and the Dandenongs. She continues to read, write, cook, bake and entertain her family and her many friends.

Top: Ernest and Marta Schwarcz and Bill, Eva, Erna and Sanyi Gross in Melbourne, circa 1952.

Bottom: At Essendon Airport to farewell Boeske, who was visiting from America, 1960.
Top row: Sanyi, Andor, Ernest.
Middle row: Erna, Baba, Boeske, Marta.
Front row: Bill, Morry, Alan, Eva.

Marta, Erna, Baba and Boeske at Essendon Airport, 1960.

The Schwartz family in the driveway of their long-term Melbourne home in Caulfield. From left: Baba, Alan, Danny, Andor, Morry.

The Schwartz family at Oscar Schwartz's bar mitzvah in 2001.
From left: Danny, Andor (who was sometimes affectionately called Bandi), Morry,
Alan and Baba.

Not in these photographs are: Baba's beloved daughters-in-law, Anna, Carol and
Uschi; Carol and Alan's children, Thea, Hannah, Oscar and Ruby; Danny's daughter,
Delilah; Thea's children, Hunter and Bonnie; and Anna's daughter, Zahava, and
grandchildren Lilith, Boaz and Hephzibah.

Coda

In 2003 Andor and Baba donated the funds to construct a memorial path, one kilometre long, in the gardens of Yad Vashem, in Jerusalem, known as the Path of Remembrance and Reflection.

Among other markers along the path, there are two private headstones. One is in memory of Andor's family: his father, Moritz; his mother, Kato; his brother, Imre; and his sister, Erszike. The other is in memory of Baba's father, Gyula.

At the consecration of this path, on the twentieth of April, 2005, in the presence of many friends, family and Israelis in public life, Baba made the following speech in which she addressed her father directly.

Survivors of the Shoah carry
An extra burden of pain, sorrow and anger.
The weight of the load does not diminish
With the passing of the years.
To Yad Vashem we come to remember,
And to relive.
So please allow me to address my father.

Father, *Apukam*, I need to speak to you.
Now that your name is engraved on that stone
I feel your immediate presence.
I feel it as strong as then, when
Our eyes met for the last time
At that accursed place at Auschwitz.

Do you remember?

Three hellish days and nights on the train of the damned,
Not enough place to sit for all of us,
You stood throughout that grim, fearful journey,
So that we could sit, your beloved ones,
Your adored wife and treasured three daughters.
You lived only for us, we were all your life.

I do remember.

We were brought to Auschwitz,
Sheep ready for slaughter.
Everything happened with lightning speed,
Men and women were separated,
Then a selection, this to right that to left.
Mother and we girls with the living were sent.

But no way for us to know to which side you went.

In a huge hall brisk orders barked:
All strip naked,
Drop your clothes where you stand.
Then inmates sheared our heads
And gave us rags to wear,
And from that shower on a warm day of May
We came out altered, humiliated, shamed.

To C Lager they took us, empty, yet to be filled,
Stood there for hours in front of our barrack.
The air was thick with smoke, the smell of burning flesh,
And old inmates told us unspeakable truth.

Then
A company of men passed, unforeseen, surprising.
I ran to see: were you amongst the men?
You wore prisoner's stripes and a prisoner cap,

Easy to recognise, you looked like your old self.
I, with boundless joy,
Arms raised called out to you:
Father, *Apukam*, look at me, here I am.
You looked at me, puzzled,
Questions rose in your eyes.
I did not know why, I did not see myself.
A crazy woman waving,
Hairless and in rags.

Do you remember?

And I kept on screaming,
Here I am look at me!
My voice did it? Perhaps,
But recognition came.
Your eyes darkened with endless sorrow,
You could not bear the sight,
Buried your face into your hands
And shuffled away, sobbing.

The last time I saw you.

I was sixteen then and you were forty-eight,
In the prime of your life, clever, capable, smart,
Lipe was with you, your wife's younger brother.

Now you looked after him,
Fed him, protected him, even in Buchenwald.

Duty bound you took him, for false promises came
From the murderers' mouth, *Y'mach Sh'mam*,
Promises of more food at a better new place.

And on the second day of Sukkot, in 1944,
They took you back to Auschwitz to be sent up in smoke,
You, and your charge, Lipe, your adored wife's brother,
With all the others.

Father, do you hear me?
Good tidings I bring you now,
From Eretz Yisrael, from Yerushalayim,
I am here to greet you, a content old woman,
By my side my husband of fifty-seven years.
He is good and clever, dutiful and caring,
With a warm heart and an open hand,
And we all love him.

Look at our three sons now, Moshe, Yechiel-Alan, Danny,
Denied the joy of having grandfathers.
They would make you so proud,
As they make us parents.
Their wives and their children

Stand beside them also.
All are strong, all are bright,
Yet loving and tender.
You would love them, I know.

I hope that you hear me,
Apukam, dear Father
Yechiel Ben Rafael Menashe
Zichroncha Livracha, Alecha Shalom

Nazi Documents from the Archive of Yad Vashem

Konzentrationslager _____ Art der Haft: _____ Gef. Nr.: 37 899

Name und Vorname: *Keimovics, Margit*

geb.: *15.III.1923.* zu: *Nyírbátor, Ungarn*

Wohnort: *Nyírbátor*

Beruf: *X*   Rel.: *israelit.*

Staatsangehörigkeit: *Ungarn*   Stand: *lled.*

Name der Eltern: *Julius K. + Erzsébet geb. Kellner* Rasse: _____

Wohnort: *Sl. Nasmits*

Name der Ehefrau: *X*

Wohnort: *X*   Rasse: _____

Kinder: *X* Alleiniger Ernährer der Familie oder der Eltern: *X*

Vorbildung: *Volksschule*

Militärdienstzeit: *X* _____ von — bis _____ *X*

Kriegsdienstzeit: *X* _____ von — bis _____ *X*

Grösse: *mittel* Nase: *normal* Haare: *braun* Gestalt: *voll*

Mund: *normal* Bart: *X* Gesicht: *rund* Ohren: _____

Sprache: *ungarisch* _____ Augen: *grau* Zähne: *gut*

Ansteckende Krankheit oder Gebrechen: _____ *X*

Besonderes Kennzeichen: _____ *keine*

Rentenempfänger: _____ *X*

Verhaftet am: *22.III.1944.* wo: *am Orte*

1. Mal eingeliefert: _____ 2. Mal eingeliefert: _____

Einweisende Dienststelle: _____

Grund: _____

Parteizugehörigkeit: _____ von — bis _____

Welche Funktionen: _____

Mitglied v. Unterorganisationen: _____

Kriminelle Vorstrafen: _____

Politische Vorstrafen: _____

Ich bin darauf hingewiesen worden, dass meine Bestrafung wegen intellektueller Urkundenfälschung erfolgt, wenn sich die obigen Angaben als falsch erweisen sollten.

v. g. u.   Der Lagerkommandant

Keimovits Margit

Stutthof arrival form for Margit Keimowitz (sic), number 37899. She gave her date of birth as 15 December 1923, adding four years to her age, pretending to be twenty-one, which she thought would enhance her chances of survival. Note the detailed physical description in this document.

Stutthof detainee personal card for Margit Keimovitcsh (sic), number 37899. Again the
physical description.

Ungar. Jude.

Konzentrationslager _____ Art der Haft: _____ Gef. Nr.: 56619

Name und Vorname: Keimovits Gyulius

geb. 27.4 .96 zu: Nyirbator Kom. Szaboles.

Wohnort: Nyirbator n.o.

Beruf: Glaser _____ Rel.: mos.

Staatsangehörigkeit: Ungar _____ Stand:

Name der Eltern: Vater: Rudolf Kaufmann verstb. 1919 Nyirbator. Rasse:

Wohnort: Mutter: Gizella geb. Grünfeld verstb. 1920 n.o.

Name der Ehefrau: Erzsebet geb. Kellner _____ Rasse:

Wohnort: K.L. Auschwitz.

Kinder: 4 /21-16/ Alleiniger Ernährer der Familie oder der Eltern:

Vorbildung: 6 Kl. Volksschule.

Militärdienstzeit: _____ von — bis

Kriegsdienstzeit: _____ von — bis 1915 - 1918

Grösse: 172 Gestalt: kräftig Gesicht: oval Augen: blau

Nase: gebogen Mund: gew. Ohren: gew. Zähne: Zellstein

Haare: blond Sprache: ungar. deutsch.

Ansteckende Krankheit oder Gebrechen:

Besondere Kennzeichen: keine,

Rentenempfänger:

Verhaftet am: 21.4.44. wo: Nyirbator

1. Mal eingeliefert 25.5.44 KL Auschwitz 2. Mal eingeliefert 2.6. 2.6.44 KL Auschwitz

Einweisende Dienststelle:

Grund:

Parteizugehörigkeit: _____ von — bis

Welche Funktionen:

Mitglied v. Unterorganisationen: keine

Kriminelle Vorstrafen: keine

Politische Vorstrafen: keine

8.10.44 KL Auschwitz

Ich bin darauf hingewiesen worden, dass meine Bestrafung wegen intellektueller Urkundenfälschung erfolgt, wenn sich die obigen Angaben als falsch erweisen sollten.

v. g. u. _____ Der Lagerkommandant

Gyulius Keimovits

KL/42/4.43 500.000

Buchenwald arrival form for Gyulius (Gyula) Keimovits, where he was provided with number 56619. The document records that he was arrested at Nyírbátor on 21 April 1944, admitted on 25 May 1944 to Auschwitz and transferred to Buchenwald on 2 June 1944. The stamp at the bottom right – '8.10.44' – indicates he was transferred again around that date to Auschwitz. At the base of the page is Gyula's signature.

Ung.-Jude.

Vor- und Zuname: Gyulius Keimovits   Haft-Nr. 56619

Beruf: Glaser   geboren am: 27.4.96 in: Nyirbator

Anschrifts-Ort: Frau: Ersebeth K., KL Au   Straße Nr.

Eingel. am: 2.6.44 Uhr von Auschwitz Entl. am 8.10.44 Uhr nach KL Auschwitz

Bei Einlieferung abgegeben:

			Koffer	Aktentasche	Paket
Hut/Mütze	Paar Schuhe/Stiefel	Kragenknöpfe	Feuerzeug		Wehrpaß
Mantel	Paar Strümpfe	Halstuch	Tabak	Pfeife	Fremdenpaß
Rock Sacko	Paar Gamaschen	Taschentuch	Zigarren/Zigaretten		Arbeitsbuch
Weste/Kletterweste	Kragen	Paar Handschuhe	Zig.-Blättchen		Invalidenkarte
Hose	Vorhemd	Brieftasche mit	Zündtuch		
Pullover	Binder/Fliege	Papiere	Messer Schere		
Oberhemden	Paar Armelhalter	Sporthemd/Hose	Bleistift/Drehbler		
Unterhemden	Paar Sockenhalter	Abzeichen	Geldbörse		
Unterhosen	Paar Mansch. Knöpfe	Schlüssel a. Ring	Komm		Wertsachen: ja—nein

Abgabe bestätigt: Effektenverwalter:

Keimovits Gyula

Another document from Buchenwald. It records that Gyula, number 56619, was transferred to Buchenwald on 2 June 1944, and was sent to Auschwitz around 8 October 1944. It too is signed by Gyula.

Gyula's card at Buchenwald. It records that Jewish prisoner number 56619 arrived from Auschwitz on 2 June 1944. The stamped date of departure is 6 October 1944. Gyula stated his profession as 'Glaser', or glazier, as he thought there were jobs in a glass factory where he knew other Jewish employees.

Ungar. Jude

Konzentrationslager

Art der Haft: _____ Gef. Nr.: 56618

Name und Vorname: KELLNER Lajos

geb.: 16.4.1906 zu: Nyirbátor, Kom. Szabolcs, Ungarn

Wohnort: Nyirbátor, w.o. Szentvér u.1.

Beruf: Glaser   Rel.: mos.

Staatsangehörigkeit: Ungarn   Stand: verh.

Name der Eltern: { Vater: Schreiber Ignácz K., z.Z. im KL. Rasse: Auschwitz.

Wohnort: { Mutter: Kornelia K., geb. Goldstein, verst. 1938 in Budapest

Name der Ehefrau: Klara K., geb. Klein   Rasse:

Wohnort: z.Z. im KL. Auschwitz

Kinder: 3 : 4, 7, 10) Alleiniger Ernährer der Familie oder der Eltern:

Vorbildung: Volksschule

Militärdienstzeit: _____ von — bis _____

Kriegsdienstzeit: _____ von — bis _____

Grösse: 163   Gestalt: mittelstark   Gesicht: eckig   Augen: braun

Nase: l. gebogen   Mund: schmal   Ohren: absteh.   Zähne: mehrere Gold z.

Haare: braun   Sprache: yiddisch, ungar.

Ansteckende Krankheit oder Gebrechen:

Besondere Kennzeichen: Narben unter d. li. Augen u. an beiden Handrücken

Rentenempfänger:

Verhaftet am: 22.4.44   wo: Nyirbátor

1. Mal eingeliefert: 25.5.44 KL. Auschwitz   überstellt   2. Mal eingeliefert: 2.6. **2.6.44** Bu.
KL Auschwitz

Einweisende Dienststelle:

Grund:

Parteizugehörigkeit: Keine   von — bis

Welche Funktionen:

Mitglied v. Unterorganisationen:

Kriminelle Vorstrafen: Keine   *8.10.44 KL Auschwitz*

Politische Vorstrafen: Keine

42404.

Ich bin darauf hingewiesen worden, dass meine Bestrafung wegen intelektueller Urkundenfälschung erfolgt, wenn sich die obigen Angaben als falsch erweisen sollten.

v. g. u.   Der Lagerkommandant

Lajos Kellner

KL/42/4.43 300.000

Lipe Kellner's arrival form from Buchenwald. Lipe was given number 56618, one number before his brother-in-law Gyula. Lipe was arrested at Nyírbátor on 22 April 1944, admitted to Auschwitz on 25 May 1944, and transferred to Buchenwald on 2 June 1944. The stamp at the bottom right – '8.10.44' – indicates he was transferred again around that date to Auschwitz. At the base of the page is Lipe's signature.

Buchenwald detainee personal card for Lajos (Lipe) Kellner, number 56618, who was transferred there from Auschwitz on 2 June 1944.

Ung.-Jude.

Vor- und Zuname:	Lajos Kellner Haft-Nr. 56618
Beruf:	Glaser geboren am: 16. 4. 06 in: Nyirbator
Anschrifts-Ort:	Frau: Klara K., KL Au. Straße Nr.
Eingel. am:	2.6.44 Uhr von Auschwitz Entl. am 3.10.44 Uhr nach Kl Auschwitz

Bei Einlieferung abgegeben:

			Koffer	Aktentasche	Paket
Hut/Mütze	Paar Schuhe/Stiefel	Kragenknöpfe	Feuerzeug	Wehrpaß	
Mantel	Paar Strümpfe	Halstuch	Tabak Pfeife	Fremdenpaß	
Rock Jacke	Paar Gamaschen Zus. Einzel	Taschentuch	Zigarren/Zigaretten	Arbeitsbuch	
Weste/Kleiderweste	Kragen	Paar Handschuhe Zus. Einzel	Zig.-Blättchen	Invalidenkarte	
Hose	Vorhemd	Brieftasche mit	Storsack		
Pullover	Binder/Fliege	Papiere	Messer Schere		
Oberhemden	Paar Armelhalter	Sporthemd/Hosen	Bleistift/Drehbleb		
Unterhemden	Paar Sockenhalter	Abzeichen	Geldbörse		
Unterhosen	Paar Wasch-Knöpfe	Schlüssel a. Ring	Kamm	Wertsachen: ja – nein	

Abgabe bestätigt   Effektenverwalter:

This Buchenwald document records that Lipe, number 56618, was transferred from Auschwitz to Buchenwald on 2 June 1944, and was returned to Auschwitz around 8 October 1944. It too is signed by Lipe.

Lipe's card at Buchenwald. It records that Jewish prisoner number 56618 arrived from Auschwitz on 2 June 1944. The stamped date of departure is 6 October 1944. Like Gyula, Lipe stated his profession as 'Glaser', or glazier.

KL-BUCHENWALD ORDNER Nr. 406

G. C. C. 2/ 256

II E/ 6

LAGERARZTUNTERSUCHUNGEN

v. 1. 9. 1944 – 31. 10. 1944

Gesamte Blattanzahl: 129

'Lagerarztuntersuchungen', or camp physician examinations. In this document, dated 30 September 1944, both Lipe and Gyula are noted as sick. A survivor of Buchenwald later told Baba that Gyula was in fact healthy at this time; he chose to go with Lipe.

55

Folgende Häftlinge sind z. Zt. für nutzbringende Arbeit nicht
einsatzfähig und zum grössten Teil behandlungsbedürftig:

16809	Moutal	53045	Moskovits	53976	Hirsch
31349	Gopolovici	53054	Prager	977	Klein
52404	Katz	11o	Löbl	998	Frenkel
437	Szasz	139	Spirer	54001	Wiegner
438	Fries	191	Gigali	975	Vizel
441	Kohn	199	Weiss	56265	Perl
444	Rosenfeld	228	Prinoz	266	Perl
449	Klein	242	Waller	3o9	Spira
45o	Klein	251	Friedman	32o	Geller
451	Katz emy	262	Deutsch	354	Muskovits
467	Friedmann	289	Noevits	363	Wieder
469	Moskovits	29o	Selczer	392	Moskovits
479	Berkovics	293	Selczer	409	Wiesel
504	Singer	313	Moskovits	541	Abraham
527	Stegman	317	Izsak	556	Berger
544	Weiss	318	Lipot	611	Mandel
55o	Arato	343	Berger	613	Müller
555	Fried	363	Reich	618	Kellner
559	Stark	392	Adler	619	Keimovits
566	Blum	393	Markbreiter	634	Jakubovics
579	Roth	4o6	Klein	637	Roth
58o	Schwartz	441	Deutsch	645	Holländer.
596	Grünberger	45o	Weiss	655	Herskovics
6o1	Gross	453	Margittai	682	Goldstein
626	Gergely	478	Grossmann	669	Klein
63o	Klein	479	Grossmann	691	Klein
633	Gross	48o	Feldman	712	Friedman
665	Deutsch	483	Bergstein	743	Paskesz
691	Sugar	487	Taub	749	Strobel
735	Weiberger	493	Lazar	754	Weinberger
739	Berger	498	Frank	774	Rosenberg
744	Pollak	504	Lukacs	791	Wechter
746	Grünstein	513	Rosenfeld	795	Gross
761	Zelig	544	Lindenfeld	8oo	Judkovics
8o9	Moses	56o	Krauss	811	Rosenberg
841	Fürszt	565	Deutsch	813	Auspitz
857	Weichselbaum	583	Staub	822	Rosenblatt
865	Fülöp	616	Klein	841	Keszler
893	Weinberg	637	Schöner	842	Frajmovits
896	Izsak	671	Weinberger	894	Mechlavits
9o2	Lefkovits	675	Finkelstein	898	Bleier
9o4	Lefkovits	679	Izsak	899	Bleier
9o7	Klein	72o	Leichtmann	9o1	Weisz
918	Braun	722	Stein	91o	Weiszer
923	Klein	725	Fried	923	Abrahamovits
925	Langer	755	Mandel	925	Fisch
927	Kramer	768	Moskovits	939	Siegel
948	Deutsch	784	Klein	966	Rasenbaum
983	Kappel	794	Wallerstein	972	Majerovits
992	Hauer	799	Epstein	974	Braunwasser
53006	Rosenzweig	817	Leithner	985	Saphir
o19	Zinstbaum	885	Mayer	57026	Rotoh
o23	Schwarcz	906	Grünfled	o29	Perl
o39	Kahan	97o	Hochstadt	o41	Gancz

54   54   54   162

The page from the above-mentioned list on which Lipe and Gyula appear.

56618

```
Kellner, Lajos                    Polit.
16.4.06 Nyirbator                 Ungar
Glaser                            Jude
   2. Juni 1944

           AUSCHWITZ  6. Okt. 1944


Wasserlauf,Leo                    Pole
geb.19.3.22 in Mähr.Ostrau        Jude
Tischler
                                  28.11.44
 14. Nov. 1944
                                   © 3
```

Document from Buchenwald recording that on 6 October 1944 Lipe was sent back to Auschwitz. There he was murdered. The number 56618 was transferred from Lipe to a new detainee, Leo Wasserlauf, who was admitted to Buchenwald on 14 November 1944.

56619

K e i m o v i t s , Gyulius   Polit.
27.4.96 Nyirbator   Ungar
Glaser   Jude
2. Juni 1944

     AUSCHWITZ   6. Okt. 1944

R i t t e r ,Naftali   Pole
geb.9.6.12 in Tarnow   Jude
Schneidermeister
14. Nov. 1944   GR   27. Nov. 1944

Document from Buchenwald recording that on 6 October 1944 Gyula was sent back to Auschwitz. There he was murdered. The number 56619 was transferred from Gyula to a new detainee, Naftali Ritter, who was admitted to Buchenwald on 14 November 1944. Naftali was sent to Gross Rosen camp on 27 November 1944.

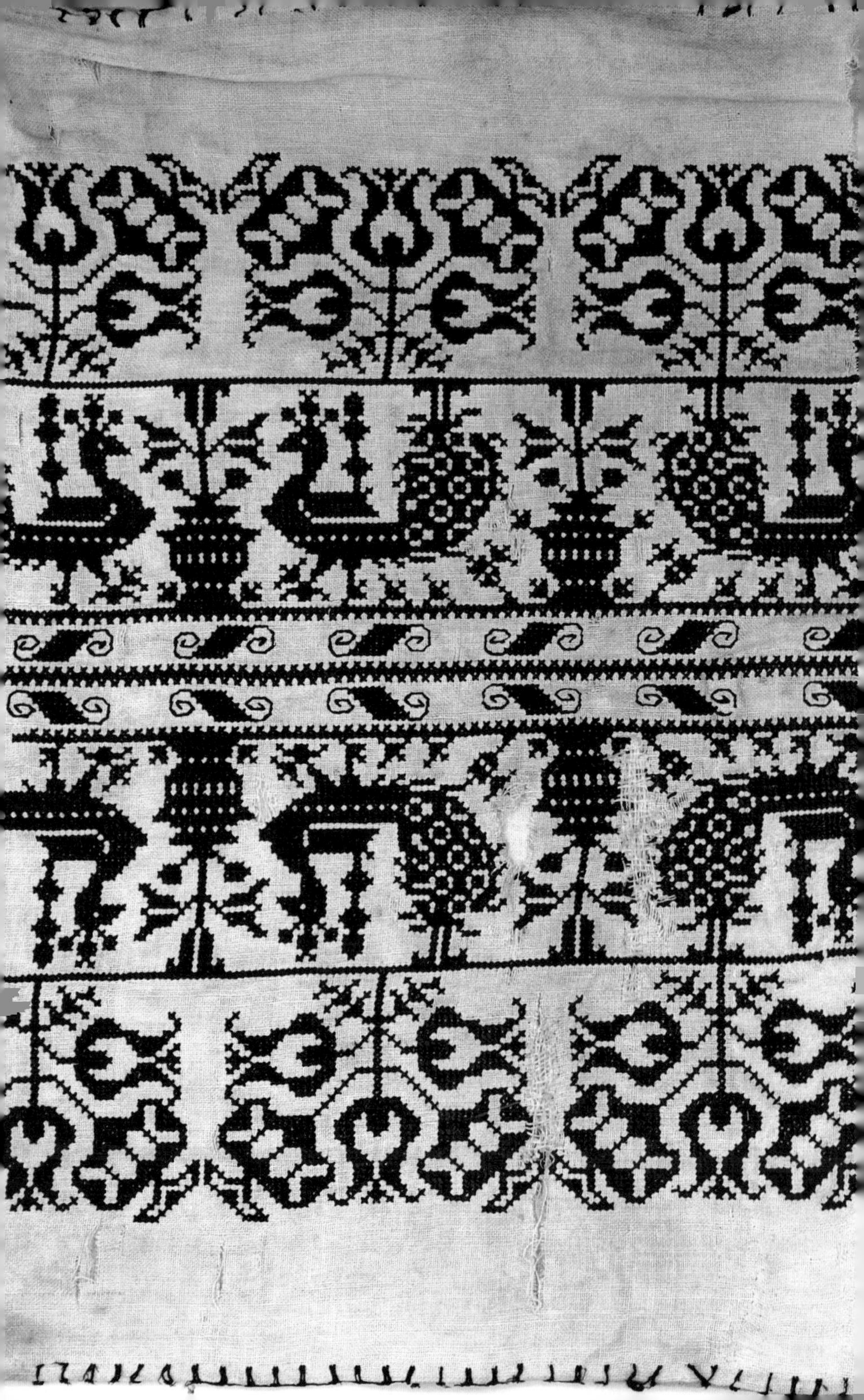